LIFE SKILLS FOR TEENS

HOW TO MANAGE EVERYDAY LIFE, INCLUDING
MONEY MANAGEMENT, SOCIAL SKILLS, STUDYING
HABITS, COOKING YOUR FAVORITE MEAL, HOW TO
CHANGE A TIRE, AND MUCH MORE.

ROBERT JAMES RYAN

ISBN: 9798376061794

CONTENTS

"Nothing comes easy while raising teenagers. Lord knows my three boys sure gave me a run for my money. In today's world, if there's any advice I could give it's this: Know where they are, know who they're with, and know what they're doing."

For my wonderful grandchildren –
Caroline, Aria, Bailee, & Colton.
You forever have my love.

INTRODUCTION

"Growing up is hard, love. Otherwise, everyone would do it."

— KIM HARRISON

It's the truth! Not everyone makes it to adulthood with the knowledge and skill set to take on the world that awaits. It's scary for all of us, but it's even worse when you aren't sure where to begin. You might be at an age where you think to yourself, "Who am I?" You're no longer a child, but you're not quite an adult yet. This in-between stage is challenging, I won't pretend like it isn't, but that's precisely why I wrote this book for you.

Are you stuck? Do you feel you're ready to grow up but don't know how to do it? Maybe you're frustrated that adults don't take you seriously or that there's a vast adventure awaiting you, but you're unsure how to leave your comfort zone. Add this to the pressures of school, a part-time job, juggling a new friend group, peer pressure, acne, and sports, and you've got quite the concoction of a nasty ball of stress. But please don't fret. Let's keep going.

Navigating high school can feel like a maze with no map, no end, and an array of impossible obstacles to overcome. This can create a feeling of uncertainty and misguidance within yourself. But what if you had a map? What if you knew the barriers you'd face before seeing them? That's what this book is going to give you; The Map. Of course, knowing every bump you'll encounter along the way is impossible. Still, the information I've provided you here will contribute to building your mental and physical strength and stamina so you can succeed and grow to reach your highest potential.

I believe I survived and succeeded in raising three rambunctious boys from their teenage years into full-fledged adulthood because of the tips and tricks I accumulated. A lot of adults today would tell you they never had a guideline laid out for them. Many of us were in the "sink or swim" category of life, and some didn't swim too well. I want you to swim. I want you to use every piece of information to your advantage so you can thrive, not just survive.

Start building your confidence today! Your emotions are valid, and your fears and aspirations are all part of your developing character. After you read this book, you'll have a more sturdy foundation to build yourself and your future. As E.E. Cummings said, "It takes courage to grow up and become who you really are." So, what are you waiting for? Get started!

GETTING TO KNOW YOU(RSELF)

*"You grow up the day you have your first real laugh –
at yourself."*

— ETHEL BARRYMORE

While it may seem slightly backward, the truth is, when you take accountability for your flaws, it's an incredible strength. We've all been embarrassed and tried to run from our fumbles, but acknowledging your weaknesses, you take your power back from anyone else who might try to cast stones. And what's a better healing tool than laughter? So let's dive into a few ways you can empower yourself and even help others do the same.

REPROGRAMING YOUR MIND

I know, I know... What does that even mean, right? Reprogramming is quite literally giving yourself the gift of, well...yourself! Growing up, we are like little sponges, mentally and emotionally soaking up information left and right. Sometimes we have experiences that might make us question our abilities, worth, or knowledge. By changing your mindset and attitude about yourself, your life becomes brighter and fuller. The best start to reprogramming is via daily affirmations: Standing alone in front of a mirror, relax your body. Don't judge yourself for how you look or your clothes. Look into your eyes and tell yourself that you are perfect exactly as you are. Tell yourself that you love yourself and that you're a wonderful, loveable person on this earth with a purpose and a destiny.

SET A GOAL THAT FITS YOU!

This is a beautiful test of intuition and follow-through. Spend some time alone and contemplate what you have the power to create. This should be something new and outside of your comfort zone. Why is this? When you set a goal for yourself, you automatically build confidence as you work towards it. Once that goal is complete, you'll be able to select the next goal, then the next, and so on. You'll look back in awe and pride at your list of accomplishments. You'll also feel less anxiety and worry about new experiences because you'll have taught yourself that you can handle challenges.

TREAT PEOPLE WELL AND BE TREATED WELL BY PEOPLE.

Letting your emotions overwhelm you when someone breaks your spirit is easy. But it's an inner strength to pull yourself up and show yourself the compassion you deserve, as well as the villain. There will always be obstacles and challenges that might bring unwanted stress, which is why protecting your energy from others is essential. You don't want an emotional vampire sucking the joy out of your soul; no one wants that from you, either. Instead, be around those who lift you and love you for exactly who you are.

TRY NEW THINGS!

There are endless possibilities of exploration waiting for you to walk through that door. A lot of life is finding new things we didn't even know existed. This book, for example, will help introduce you to a variety of different things you get to try for the first time. Remember that no one was good at anything they tried the first time. We're humans, we're not meant to be perfect. But we should try our best at everything we do and build well-earned self-esteem.

WHAT DO YOU DO WELL? -NOW, DO IT!

You have talents that you may not even realize are special about you, but there are things you can do that no one else can. First, spend some time getting to know your values and priorities. What lights you up from the inside out? Look inside yourself, don't look at the person next to you, and locate your strengths. Now lean into them! Cultivating the specific skills that are meaningful to you will fulfill you in a way that imitating someone else never will.

THE PERSON WHO NEEDS YOUR COMPASSION THE MOST IS YOU.

In a world where we compare and criticize each other to death, it can tire us to the bone. It's tough when you're in the transitional teenage years when you're trying to figure everything out. You want all the answers right away and you want to be accepted by your family, adults, and friends. But let's not forget something: Everyone feels lost at some point. Your job is never to be perfect, popular, or cool. Your job is to love yourself unconditionally. The only person who has permission to be in your head is yourself. So, make sure your words and thoughts are helping, loving, and caring.

PRACTICE POSITIVE SELF-TALK.

There's always a voice in your head guiding you with every step you take. That voice is under the direct control of YOU. Ask yourself this: "Do I feel more confident and capable of completing a task when someone yells at me and tells me I'm stupid?" -I bet the answer was "NO!" Because if you feel better about yourself when other people respect you, then you must treat yourself with that respect. The things we say to ourselves create intentions that manifest as energy in our bodies. Set up your intentions to HELP, not HARM you. Giving yourself positive feedback and encouragement will not only make you happier, but it will also help you accomplish more of those goals you're setting for yourself along the way.

AH, YES...JOURNALING! A FAVORITE STRESS-REDUCER.

Did you know that your brain only likes to focus on one thing at once? When you're troubled about something and feel like you can't figure out a good solution, journaling is a beautiful way to escape and bring attention back to positive thoughts. The trick to journaling is never to judge what you're writing. I recommend grabbing a fun journal that fits your personality and always keeping it with you. When you need to get something out, write it down. Remember that these are your private thoughts, and no one will see them (just keep the journal somewhere safe). There will not be a grade for this. Your journal is just another place for your thoughts to live. To get started, I suggest listing ten strengths, daily affirmations, ten accomplishments, and ten things for which you're grateful. You will feel better.

WHAT HAS COMPARING YOURSELF TO OTHERS EVER GOTTEN YOU?

It's easy to say we don't compare ourselves to others, but we all indeed do it. And with the explosion of social media, it's no wonder self-esteem can dip so low when every other person is an IG model or an influencer. But please remember who you are and where you are. No one else is you and no one else is exactly where you are at this moment. You are unique unto yourself. Comparing yourself to another person only creates envy and takes you away from focusing on the importance of levelling up in your own life. When you're on social media and you feel that pang of envy in your chest, immediately stop, look at yourself, name your best qualities (yes, you have a lot), and give the ego boost to yourself, not someone else!

THERE'S NO SUCH THING AS PERFECT.

Of course, it's good to put your best foot forward and try your best. But don't confuse your best with striving for perfection. The idea of perfection is just that, it's an idea. And not only is it subjective, but it's an impossible standard to meet. So instead, be proud of your best. Acknowledge your accomplishments for precisely what they are. If you tried hard and gave it your all, then that's an achievement on its own.

FOCUS ON YOUR EFFORT, NOT THE OUTCOME.

Getting wrapped up in the desired outcome goes back to perfectionism. Yes, it would be best to have a solid and realistic goal when working on any project. However, it can be all too easy to lose yourself in the tunnel vision of the expected outcome that you don't even focus on the work it takes to get there. Instead, begin by imagining what you'd like to achieve and then take the steps one by one to get there. For example, say you're writing an essay, and you know you want a B. The essay doesn't just appear out of thin air. You must type one word after the other in an order that makes sense to the storyline and structure. You'll also need good grammar, spelling, and punctuation to obtain a good grade. This is the focus I'm talking about. If you set a goal to work toward, take your time and enjoy the process. The outcome might be even better than you'd anticipated.

FOCUS ON WHAT GOES WELL.

It's only human to get swept away in our daily worries and problems, but we lose sight of the good stuff when we trap ourselves in a hostile mental prison. You'll have rough days, and that's life, but balance the bad with the good. Find a few good things that happened to you that day, too. Every experience is a learning opportunity for growth, and I'd say that's even more true for our negative experiences. Spending time focusing on specific skills you have confidence and strength in can also help bring you out of a rut.

GIVE AND HELP (ESPECIALLY STRANGERS)

The gift of giving is vital to building empathy for others, especially strangers, from whom you will not expect anything in return. Creating your internal moral compass takes practice, and helping others doesn't just give them a leg up, but it will make you feel good, also. Seeing the difference, you make in someone's life or day will boost your self-esteem, and you'll learn that you can find joy without receiving anything back.

TAKE CARE OF YOUR BODY!

Your body is your house; no, we're talking about your TEMPLE here! Practicing self-care isn't an option but a requirement for confidence and success. The goal isn't to look like Arnold Schwarzenegger but to balance your whole body, mind, and spirit. Eating foods high in nutrients will make you healthier and stronger. Physical exercise improves body image and naturally boosts your immune system. Meditation can be done anywhere, anytime; you need the breath in your lungs and a clear, calm mind to end negative thoughts or emotions. Sleep is CRUCIAL! So many teens are sleep deprived and might not even realize that 8 hours of sleep at night can create a natural sense of optimism. All this combined gives you the best shot at completing your life goals.

EXPLORE YOUR NEEDS.

Before diving headfirst into dreaming up the career and life we want for ourselves, first thing's first: What do you need to feel balanced and whole? We love the ones who raised us, but we also realize that we are individuals. Each of us requires our needs met to bolster our confidence. Six human needs are as follows: *Significance* in the world and recognizing our uniqueness. *Connection/Love* to bond and unite with others to develop emotions and empathy. *Certainty* can assure us that, at times when we can experience pleasure and avoid pain. *Variety* expands our neuro-pathways to build from new stimulatory experiences. *Contribution* will allow us to help, support and give selflessly to others when appropriate. And last but not least, *Growth* expands our perspectives, allowing our capacity for inevitable life changes to strengthen us.

TAKE NOTE OF YOUR INTERESTS

One roadblock teenagers tend to face is the ability to discover their true interests and talents. Your passions as a child are shifting and might be completely different than they are now. But it's hard to know what you're good at or your career or hobby interests if you don't try new things. A benefit to using social media or the internet is the wide variety of experiences, cultures, and vocations you have available to explore at your fingertips. The aim is to be realistic in your search. Think of something you enjoy and would like to dig deeper to expand your career possibilities. An example would be if you love modern art but aren't skilled as an artist. You might not become a world-famous artist, but architecture might be a fantastic career path that allows you to tap into your creative side while providing a stable financial foundation for your life.

CHILL FOR A BIT AND RELAX.

Anxieties and fears- in small doses-are a part of life that is necessary to examine our priorities and life paths. But too much can get out of hand and lead to a miserable life. Daily routines to relax are just as important as showering and eating a balanced diet. When I say relax, I don't mean to lie on the couch and scroll through Twitter because your brain is still engaged, even if you don't know it. Relaxing your mind and body even a few minutes a day can help alleviate too much anxiety and fear when they get out of hand. The nice thing is you can do this anywhere. Find a comfortable position to sit still, close your eyes, and clear your mind. Other relaxation practices could be spending an extra ten minutes walking the dog or taking a hot bath. The intention should be to calm your mind and body, so however you do that is up to you!

NOTICE THE PATTERNS.

Our brains love to have patterns to work from and habits to form. It's a way for our bodies to protect themselves and survive. As I mentioned earlier, steering ourselves away from negative thought patterns will defend us from choosing harmful behaviours which can lead to poor consequences. Our positive mind states can tell us a lot about what our bodies need to develop and achieve balance at that time. For example, if you feel the urge to go driving with friends on the weekends, you might be exploring new life experiences. If you find yourself drawn to a particular movie genre, it could mean you're finding inspiration that you could somehow use in your life. Take note of the habits you're forming now. A conscious awareness of these patterns could help you explore yourself deeper.

ANALYZE YOUR FEARS.

Following up with the point above about noticing patterns, we're going to experience fear. It can be a new fear, or it can be developed-yes as a pattern. Think about a time you felt fear and immediately wanted to quit something because of that feeling. Fear is a primitive response to keep us safe from harm. However, we can also feel fear when we come across something new and unknown that isn't damaging but maybe something that makes us question our capabilities and confidence. Learning to identify this emotion can help you to overcome it.

Steps to combat fear: 1. Identify fear for what it is when you feel it. 2. See that you can use this fear to create positive momentum. 3. Listen to your fear. Why is it there? Allow yourself to feel it and become familiar with it. 4. Set goals that help you overcome these fears. Take a leap of faith! 5. Did you make an excuse to get out of doing number 4? LOL. I get it. But try to recognize when you're making excuses. You're only slowing your progress. 6. Surround yourself with successful peers 7. Develop a desire for growth! 8. There is an insight to be found in your pain. This can be valuable to your growth. 9. Go ahead and set a few goals to be worth it through fear. 10. Accept your failures as inevitable ways to become stronger.

YOU-NIQUE TALENTS.

Yes, you're unique. There are over 7 billion humans on the planet, and only ONE of you is alive. Incredible isn't it?! This is a time you're meant to explore yourself, so if you don't know exactly who you're meant to be, don't worry! Try some extracurricular activities at school or reach-put programs through your local government. Try as many different things as possible, and no, you're not going to be great at everything. But you'll never know where your passions lie if you don't put forth the effort! Now is a great time to face those fears we talked about to achieve optimum growth.

ACCEPT THE CHALLENGE: GET OUT OF YOUR COMFORT ZONE!

Time to open that beautiful brain of yours! Comfort is, well, comfy. But we don't develop when we become apathetic or complacent. Expanding your comfort zone is the number one way to meet new people and enjoy the art of adventure. But where do you start?

Here are a few ways to start: 1. Change your daily, weekly, and monthly routines. 2. Try something completely new, like drawing, learning to play an instrument, skateboarding, reading a random book, or any new activity to which you're drawn. 3. Try out or apply for a leadership position in a social, sports, or school club. 4. Volunteer for a passionate cause. 5. Start exercising! 6. Question the "WHY" in everything you do. 7. Face more fears.

GET A PART-TIME JOB.

While you're discovering yourself in school and extracurricular activities, finding a part-time job can add to the teenage experience. A job is a great way to create a character for yourself and learn money management and independence. A part-time job will also allow you to get the hang of the real world and how a workplace, bosses, colleagues, and schedules operate. This structure is excellent, and getting a paycheck you earned for yourself is a tremendous feeling of accomplishment.

DEFINING PEER PRESSURE.

By your age, I'm sure you've heard the term "peer pressure" mentioned more than once, and for a good reason! Peer pressure can creep up anywhere you interact with other teenagers in any setting, from school or church youth groups to boy or girl scouts. The feeling you get from being pressured into doing something by your peers can make you feel stuck between a rock and a hard place. You're at a point where you want to meet new friends and have new experiences, so it's hard to say "No" to something you're uncomfortable with when you're being pushed into doing it. Peer pressure can come across in a direct form, such as a classmate offering you a joint behind the school gym. When you refuse, they tell you you're lame and to go away, so your ego kicks in and immediately wants to prove that you're not lame, so you smoke it too. But keep in mind that peer pressure may not be so direct. Peer pressure can show up in the form of manipulation. The commonly referred phrase of "..but everybody's doing it" implies that you're an outcast if you don't participate in whatever you're being pushed into doing. Here are a few examples of peer pressure, but keep in mind that peer pressure can be for anything you're uncomfortable with or without your consent.

1. Having sex/sexting.
2. Using alcohol/drugs.
3. Stealing/deception/lying/cheating
4. Skipping school/responsibilities

5. Submitting plagiarised work
6. Pushed to behave in a way that is not authentic to yourself.

Peer pressure can be summed up as another person trying to take away your ability to control yourself, which may lead to dishonoring your beliefs.

REASONS TO SAY NO.

There are a lot of choices you're going to make in life, and your teenage years are when you start this practice. As a teen who's trying to learn themselves, trying new experiences that are fun and can catalyze growth is one thing. Defying your intuition just to be accepted by another person is NOT a reason to agree. If you're being pushed or prodded into doing something you don't feel good about, ask yourself if there's a benefit. Are the consequences of your actions going to help you or hurt you? At the end of the day, who are you living your life for, them or you? As painful and challenging as it might be to get the words out, if you're put in a position to dishonor yourself, then the answer is "no." I don't care if your knees shake and you sweat through your t-shirt. You're going to be OK, and you can politely say with confidence, "I can make my own choices, thanks." Because the only person who is in control of you is YOU. Don't give your power away to other people. Leaders learn to protect their energy, not hurt it. Sometimes using deflective humor might work if you feel more comfortable.

Just make sure your message is clear.

UGH…. BULLIES. HOW TO DEAL WITH THEM.

I wish I could tell you that bullies cease to exist once you leave your teenage years and enter adulthood, but unfortunately, that wouldn't be true. When you think of a bully, maybe you imagine Sid from Toy Story, the classic mean guy with the mohawk blowing up small toys and picking on other kids. The Sids of the world exist, but you should be aware of different types of bullying, too. Physical bullying can happen, especially in places where authority figures aren't present, like locker rooms or unsupervised parties.

There's also verbal, cyber, relationship, and workplace bullying. When you feel like someone is trying to intimidate, control, disempower, or manipulate you, there are a few things to know about these people. First, there's something wrong with them. Yes, I know it's harsh, but it's true. There's a lot of psychology that goes into distinguishing different mental health disorders, but one thing bullies share is the need for control or power. Often, these personalities develop because of a lack of boundaries and control in their lives at home. On the exterior, they present a mask of superiority and toughness, but on the inside is a lot of self-loathing and pain. Their behavior towards you is a projection of their issues as a way to release this pain from themselves by putting it onto someone else. When they feel a lack of control in their own lives at home, they will try to control their surroundings and other people to create a false sense of security.

Nothing you did and nothing you'll ever do is never your fault for how they treat you. However, a few things are essential to keep yourself as safe as possible if you find yourself in one of these situations.

1. Do NOT bully them back. Aggression towards them only throws fuel on the fire because you've given them control over you by reacting.
2. Use the "Grey Rock Method." Be as bored, uninterested, and unemotional as possible. Show them that they're so dull that you've turned to stone from boredom.
3. If you need to run for help, run for help. I'm serious. Now isn't a time to develop a hero complex. Instead, find someone who can help you if you or another person is in harm's way.

4. If you're going somewhere public, go in a group if you can.
5. If you've got a sense of humor, use it. It'll distract them.
6. If cyberbullied, BLOCK them. Bye-bye, thanks. And don't come back! Change passwords, and don't give them ANY personal information.
7. Tell an adult immediately.

If you aren't sure you're being bullied, ask yourself if you feel good during or after the interaction. If you feel worn down, tired, depleted, or drained, you may be dealing with an emotionally abusive person. Remove yourself from these situations to maintain the balance you've been working so hard to achieve. And never feel ashamed to ask for help.

Learning about your needs, desires, and habits can take some practice, but I think you will enjoy exploring yourself. Everything we've discussed so far has led you to a place where you can think about where you want to go in life and how you can get there using discernment and intuition. Use these guidelines to develop yourself into the strongest leader teen you can be. While you're embarking on this journey toward adulthood, this brings us to our next topic of discussion: tie everything you learned by *Honing Healthy Habits.*

HONING HEALTHY HABITS

"Discipline is choosing between what you want now and what you want most."

— ABRAHAM LINCOLN.

MAKE A TIME-MANAGEMENT PLAN.

While I invite you to enjoy the newness of this time in your life and to discover passions and creativity, it's also time to invest in your responsibilities. Learning anything new is hard, but when balancing school life with social life, time might feel against you. Accomplishing what's necessary to move ahead is a MUST, so let's set you up for success instead of failure. But why is time management critical, especially if it feels like adults are conducting your life? Well, because they're not going to oversee your schedule when you're off on your own. Set yourself up on a routine that encourages academic success while giving you enough personal space for activities, resting, and working a part-time job.

First, start by assessing your time to get a good overview of your current schedule. Now think of ways to streamline your productivity in all areas. Here are some time-management skills to consider:

1. Wake up earlier. This way, you can add extra time back into your day.
2. Grab a weekly planner and write down your schedule. Then find the areas where you can map out your free time and begin filling in those gaps appropriately.
3. Create a feasible routine. Don't stretch yourself too thin. Work your way into a developed routine over a few months so as not to lead to burnout.
4. Find an environment that's best to complete your work.
5. If you don't have time for something, be OK with saying "no."

6. Find a watch you love and wear it every day. Please put it on immediately after you shower, so you don't forget it.
7. Develop good study habits. Studying needs to take up enough time in your day to let the information you're learning sink in. Make sure you're updated on the expectations and deadlines of all assignments, and add these to your calendar or weekly planner.
8. Take breaks! After 90 minutes, get some water and food, and walk around.

GET INTO EXERCISING!

Our bodies are made for movement, so engaging in physical activities is a must. Muscle-strengthening exercises and cardio build up our bodies, and it's also proven to strengthen our minds. Strenuous movement releases reward-based hormones that make us happier, live longer, and help our bodies develop. So, before you jump off your couch and head to the nearest gym, there are some things you should know before diving in-, maybe even literally. As with all things, moderation is vital to creating a healthy workout routine.

There are many physiological differences between cardio and weightlifting/strengthing exercises that would take an entire book to explain. And there is! It's in your anatomy and physiology course around junior high school. But for now, let's touch on some basic movements to get you started. Cardio can help build the endurance of your heart and vasculature by engaging in things like running, using an elliptical, or a stair climber. Weightlifting will target your muscles to build them up stronger and have better resistance. Your immune system will also significantly boost, especially from weight-bearing workouts.

Tips for Exercising.

I can't say this loud enough, so here it is for the kids in the back:

"EFFORT > PERFORMANCE!!"

I'm stressing this point for two reasons: 1. You're only here to compete with yourself, not others. If you overdo it and get injured, you'll scare yourself from wanting to work out. 2. Your body is different than every single person's body on this planet. If you're putting forth your best effort, that's hitting the goal, and now you've just won! Also, ensure you're breathing the entire time, emphasizing NOT holding your breath. Finally, it's up to you to pick a workout routine you enjoy the most. It's incredible fun once you get into it, I promise. Here are a few exercises you can look up and try on your own (or in a group) to get you started.

Back to Basics: Let's get you started at square one with some bodyweight exercises to get you warmed up and used to the movements and positions.

- Forward, side, and backward lunges
- Sit-ups (Tuck your feet under a couch to keep yourself anchored)
- Push-ups (keep your elbows tucked in, not pointed out)
- Squats (head looking straight ahead. Only go down to a sitting position)
- Chair squats (squat down into a sitting position on a chair to get good form)
- Butterfly kicks (Lie on your back, hands supporting your lower back, and flutter kick)
- Hip bridges (Lie on your back, arms to your sides, bend your knees, and raise your hips)

Pro tip: Don't focus on how your body looks or how you want it to look. If you're starting out, just get used to doing the movements correctly. The six-pack abs and quad sweep will happen eventually, especially when you pair it with a healthy eating lifestyle.

Sweat it Out.

Once you've mastered the basics, you can move into more brisk activities. Here are some to get you started.

- Pleasure walking (fast-paced walking can be done in the woods or on a sidewalk)
- Climbing stairs (more intensive cardio and leg workout to be done at home or a gym)
- Dancing!! (You can dance at home or try a Zumba class)

Picking Up the Pace.

Once you start feeling bored with the more straightforward routines, you know you've hit your reasonable exercise goal. Congratulations! You can still use your favorite parts as a warm-up for more advanced workouts. More advanced exercises are listed here for you, but remember that you can create any routine that you find fun and gets you a healthy mind and body.

- Power walking and running
- Swimming (join a team if there's one available to you)
- Cycling
- Roller skating

- Jumping rope
- Gymnastics
- Hiking (this is harder than you'd think, but so much fun)
- Soccer
- Football
- Weightlifting

Pro tip: There are apps available to download that can help you find exercises targeting specific areas of the body. A great app that I use and recommend is called JEFit. It breaks the musculature down into groups and gives each group a detailed list of exercises—this way, you know how to do the movements correctly to optimize performance.

Your aim should be to do some exercise every day, and it really is the effort that counts. Get your heart and blood pumping for 30 minutes a day. Feel your endorphins kick in and congratulate yourself on putting this kind of self-care on your list of priorities.

SLEEP...ZZZZZZZZZZZZZZZ....

Not even gonna lie about it; sleeping might be my number 1 favorite hobby now that I'm older. But as a teenager, we have so many things on our minds that sleep doesn't get prioritized the way it should. Nowadays, I can say I get 9 hours of solid rest every night, but when I was in my teenage years, it was probably more like 5. A lot of research shows that people your age need between 8 and ten hours of sleep every night to prevent the effects of sleep deprivation. Your mind and body are no longer that of a child's, and it's growing and transforming rapidly. There is also the enormous weight of your new responsibilities and interests. Getting the right amount of rest is not an option. It's a requirement. So, what does life look like when you don't get enough sleep? Sleep deprivation can manifest in many forms, all of which are negative. Some examples include the inability to concentrate, poor memory, depression/anxiety, slow reflexes, poor academic and social performance, risky behavior and lack of self-confidence, frequent/repetitive illnesses, and feeling like crap in general. With the proper amount of sleep, these negatives will be reversed and help create a balanced and pleasant day-to-day life.

How to Prevent Sleep Deprivation.

Hey, make sure you give yourself a break if you find it difficult to turn off your brain at night. Not only do you have a lot going on, but you have hormone fluctuations causing chaos. And even if you don't want to, your parents are likely telling you to put away electronics or anything with a screen. When you aren't actively engaged in studying, remember that your brain is still processing information when stimulated. Getting a break from screens 30 minutes before you get into bed can help your brain unwind. Try to get into bed around the same time every night, even on the weekends. I cringe saying this, but it's true; sleeping in on weekends can throw you off your game the entire week. Now, this is up to you because sleeping in on weekends can catch you up on sleep, but it will be harder to fall asleep at your normal time. It'll also make you groggy Monday morning when you're back to your school schedule. This is a great time to practice using discernment.

If you choose not to stick to the same sleep schedule every night and the same wake-up time in the mornings (which I recommend), then consider trying a few of the following tips.

Sleep Tips:

1. Get in bed early on Sunday night to prepare for Monday morning.
2. Be mature enough to turn off your cell phones/tablets/laptops/etc. at a reasonable time without being asked by your parent. This

will also go a long way in showing them that you're becoming responsible on your own.

3. Ask your parents not to schedule early morning appointments/meetings/events for you on the weekends.

4. Ask your parents to help you form a daily, weekly, and monthly schedule. It will show them how seriously you're taking your responsibilities, and they will feel like they can trust you to make good decisions for yourself.

5. Take a nap in the afternoon, but no longer than 30 minutes. Otherwise, it could be challenging to fall asleep at night.

6. Avoid drinking soda, coffee, tea, or any other stimulating beverage past noon.

If you're still struggling to get enough sleep, make a bedtime routine that coaxes you into a soothing and relaxing mode. Say you decide to sleep at 8 pm with a 5 am wake up. That means setting the alarm no later than 7:30 pm as a reminder to get away from screens. But beyond avoiding screen time, make a routine and stick to it -firmly- for 21 days. This is the number of days research has shown to develop a habit or routine. After that, you can decide if you want to meditate to clear your mind before bed, or maybe you'd prefer to drink a warm glass of milk. Make sure your bedroom is quiet, dark, and safe. Try not to get into bed any other time during the day unless you're sleeping. This is because you want to train your brain to associate your bed with sleep. That way, when you hit the sheets, you've created a pattern in your brain telling you it's rest time.

Pro Tip: Exercising during the day will require extra rest for your body. Studying and psychological engagements will demand extra rest of your mind. With this combination in balance, you can find it not only easier to get enough sleep for yourself, but you'll look forward to it.

DEALING WITH STRESS.

I bet the whole world agrees when I say that dealing with stress is one of the most complicated challenges you'll face. It can – and probably will -- show up in almost every situation and can be caused by absolutely anything. One of the trickiest parts of identifying stress as an emotion is that it feels different for everyone. And not only does it feel different, one thing that causes me stress might not be something that causes stress for you. When I start to feel that sinking black hole inside my chest, I ask, "WHY do I feel this, and is it justified?" Now, hold on, because I don't want you to think that I'm asking you to talk yourself out of your feelings, because I'm not. In fact, I'm asking that you lean into them to figure out what is causing you distress so you can determine the best ways to handle it. As I said, stress manifests differently for everyone, but there are some common symptoms I'm going to list for you.

Common Symptoms of Stress.

1. Nervous or anxious feelings.
2. Feeling tired frequently
3. Chest pains and stomach aches
4. Procrastination or responsibility neglect
5. Feeling overwhelmed
6. Up and down mood swings (hormone fluctuations can cause this too)
7. Recurring negative feelings/thoughts
8. Withdrawing from pleasurable experiences/family/friends
9. Sleeping issues (too much or too little)
10. Difficulties focusing, remembering, or concentrating
11. Attraction to self-medicating substances to "numb," such as alcohol or drugs
12. New and random physical ailments

You may feel some of these stress symptoms, or you may feel stress in other ways I've not mentioned. You must learn to listen to your body and respect what it's trying to tell you. As I said in chapter one, stress is an innate mechanism to protect us from harm. Stress can sometimes be a good thing, like when you're getting ready to take an exam. As always, in moderation, your heightened senses increase blood flow, and your heart rate can sharpen your focus. When stress –both good and bad-- isn't managed correctly that physiological and psychological symptoms can manifest, impacting your life in some not-so-fun ways. So, what are the steps to personally managing stress when it arises?

1. Identify the cause of the problem and acknowledge what it is head-on.
2. Avoid unnecessary stressful situations when possible. But, of course, you're not going to escape every stressor, so we'll cover some techniques to combat unavoidable stress.
3. Let things go that no longer serve you. For example, if something happened in the past and there's nothing you can do about it now, practice letting it go. Use it as a learning experience and focus on how you'd handle that situation in the future so you don't have the same issues.

4. Continue taking care of your body, mind, and spirit.
5. Eat healthy meals
6. Sleep well

ALLOW YOURSELF TO FEEL YOUR EMOTIONS.

There's an untrue stigma surrounding emotions, that feeling or showing them is a sign of weakness, and that just isn't true. Your emotions are just as essential to your body's health and well-being as any other natural body process. OK, this might be gross but hear me out. If you needed to use the bathroom, but someone told you to hold it and never to go because if you did, that would make you weak, would you listen? Probably not. Why? Because it's natural and downright crazy, plus impossible. Just as it's impossible never to pee again, it's also impossible not to have emotions, including crying, to release built-up tension and stress.

When we don't express ourselves for fear of rejection or persecution, it can lead to "masking." The concept of masking is that you hold your true feelings on the inside but project a false image on the outside to avoid embarrassment or to gain acceptance. You might eventually grow bitter and resentful of needing to wear this mask for others, which often leads to mental health disorders or pathologies later in life. All this ties back to honoring yourself and trusting your gut. If you would rather be fake about who you are to be "liked" by someone(s), then you should know that 1. Those people aren't your people, and 2. They don't deserve you. It's clique to say, "Be Yourself," especially when you're still trying to figure that out. However, your soul knows who you are, so listen to your intuition.

Emotions can range from euphoria to despair, and you will experience the full spectrum many times. You're going to learn from both the bad and the good. But when you're trapped in the bad, please take some time to sit with yourself and get to know what your body is asking of you. Sit or lie somewhere comfortable, and relax all your muscles, starting from your head and neck and then all the way to your toes. Let your body become supported by a chair or couch and close your eyes. Breathe slowly through your nose, letting your belly rise, paying attention only to your breath. Then let the air out of your lungs through your mouth. Do this for several minutes, clearing your mind and bringing your awareness to your body and breathing. Finally, acknowledge your feelings and release intense emotions.

Balancing your time, health, wellness, and emotions can be difficult. Give yourself grace as you learn to maneuver through these tricky obstacles, and learn to love yourself exactly as you are. We're all a work-in-progress, and there's no need to feel rushed through any of it. Instead, you become the best, most authentic version of yourself and watch as you surpass all your expectations. Now that you know what you want from yourself and the possibilities that await you, let's introduce you to the next step in your journey: *Strengthening Your Social Skills.*

If you or someone you know is raising kids in this fast-paced, crazy world of technology and peer pressure, then you also know how imperative it is to get them started in the right direction. Life Skills for Teens is here as a guide to help navigate these tough years by giving them the tools they need to pave the best future possible.

Scroll up, click "Buy Now with 1-Click," and Get Them Reading TODAY!

STRENGTHEN YOUR SOCIAL SKILLS

"If you go looking for a friend, you're going to find they're very scarce. If you go out to be a friend, you'll find them everywhere."

— ZIG ZIGLAR.

MAKING FRIENDS

Now that you've spent some time getting to know yourself and learning to self-soothe in the previous chapters, we'll use your authenticity to make new friends. It's true that we need time alone, but we are social animals who find joy and stability in the bonds we form with others. But now that you're out of childhood, making friends isn't quite as simple as bouncing about on a jungle gym or play dates set by your parents. So now that you're taking on new-found independence and expanding your way of thinking, you're going to be more selective in your friend group – or at least you should be.

If you grew up going to the same school, it might be challenging to meet new people. Maybe you're already familiar with everyone in your class, but you can feel the pull to find new souls with whom you can connect. That's just an example. After all, it doesn't matter where you grew up because meeting new and exciting people is always fun to expand your views and perspectives. Here are some excellent ways to social branch out.

1. Join extracurricular activities! I've already said this before, but I'm repeating it. After the school day ends, find something that you genuinely want to do. I say it this way because there's no point in forcing yourself into an activity in which you have no interest. For example, join an art class if you're drawn to art. If you're into chess, join a chess club. Making friends in an environment where you have shared interests will be easier.

2. Attend get-togethers and parties. I understand the anxiety that can creep in when you're invited to a party or event. The pressure to "perform" might hit you out of nowhere but remember that this isn't an interview. You aren't going to be on a stage trying to win the affections of the crowd like a jester. Look at it this way: You're going to interview THEM for the position of being your friend, not the other way around. So stand in your power and your truth. You're fantastic, and the right people will think so too.

3. Host get-togethers. Seriously, please do it. Who doesn't want home game advantage? And it doesn't need to be on your property. You could choose to invite some friends out to the movies, go shopping at a mall, or out to watch sports. By including your peers, you show your integrity by treating others how you want to be treated.

4. Volunteer!! There are a few ways volunteering will benefit you: You're going to meet new people outside your usual crowd. And giving back to the community in some way can make you feel great about yourself; it looks great on a college application.

5. Find a part-time job! I spoke about this before, but this is your friendly reminder that this is a great tool for personal development. Some of my favorite and longest-running friendships are from my various jobs as a teenager. There's something about the experience of working together that bonds you together.

6. Communicate clearly and honestly! It's a clique, but it's good: "Say what you mean and mean what you say." You want to trust what others say or do, so do them a favor and lead by example. Besides, you feel good about yourself when you speak your truth, and you feel like garbage when you don't. Let's revisit stress management for a minute. If you feel angry, stressed, or upset with a friend, do NOT gossip or complain about them to other friends or peers. While it may "get it off your chest," for a minute, you've just done a lot of damage to that person and now tarnished your reputation.

Try your best to communicate honestly about your feelings to others. It's a learning curve, so give yourself and them lots of much-needed patience. Everyone is in the same boat trying to navigate these rough waters, so hold on tight while you work through this.

If you ever feel nervous in any situation, especially socially, remember that they feel that way too! To get you started on the best way to communicate, here is a list to break down the steps to having a conversation.

THE BASICS OF A CONVERSATION.

1. Be polite but enthusiastic when you enter a conversation. Be approachable, not dominating.
2. Introduce yourself! It's OK to be shy at first, but let's get you started by sharing who you are.
3. Starting a conversation might feel intimidating, and it's easy to overthink. Food for thought: I've never had bad luck when sharing a genuine compliment with someone. When I was a freshman in high school, I was walking by another guy who had on a leather coat I liked. So, as I was passing him, I said, "hey, that's a nice jacket." I wasn't stopping to chat, but he immediately responded by saying, "thanks, I got it at (some local store in our hometown)." I nodded and said, "nice." When I saw him in the gym later that week, picking up a conversation without feeling awkward was easy.
4. Make eye contact with the person with whom you're speaking. It's polite and tells them your focus is on them, not somewhere else.

5. Speak clearly and loudly enough for them to hear you. Nerves might be making you shy at first, and that's OK. Keep yourself calm by reminding yourself that you're a good person with good intentions.

6. Accept the different opinions of others. You're unique, but so are they. Everyone is going to have their reality based on the experiences they've had in life. They're allowed to have different backgrounds, thus different opinions on various subjects. Now is a time to learn from others, not fight with them. Engaging in a friendly debate is healthy. Arguing or telling someone they're wrong is not.

7. Don't interrupt anyone...EVER. I don't care what they're saying to you. You're going to be a stronger, bigger person for letting the other person complete what they say. Likewise, if you're speaking and someone interrupts you, kindly ask them to wait until you're finished. It's about communicating! What an excellent way to exercise your right to boundaries and to learn to respect the boundaries of others.

THE DREADED, AWKWARD...-CRICKETS-....SILENCE.

In case you were wondering why a lull mid-conversation can feel so awkward, it all stems from our hunter-gatherer roots. Our ability to socialize allowed us to stay within the tribe. Therefore, we had protection and safety from the harsh and scary world our ancestors endured at that time. So, when you feel awkward silence and panic in your belly, gently remind yourself that it's normal.

It's inevitable. At some point, you'll be in a conversation that extends past its natural endpoint. So to avoid that odd sensation and situation in the future, here are a few key factors to straighten it out.

1. As I mentioned in the story about the boy's jacket, give a sincere compliment and/or ask a question.
2. Ask them for a story, not an answer. For example, if I asked you, "Why do you play guitar?" that may feel like a question that puts the other person on the spot. You might not mean it this way, but it could appear accusatory. Like, "ew, guitar? Really?" The other person might feel the need to defend why they play guitar. Instead, you're asking, "Hey, that's

awesome you play guitar. How did you get started?" Now you have a genuine question and the ability for the person you're asking to give a story that you two can connect through. See the difference?

3. Read the situation. Turn on that intuition of yours! You never know what someone is going through in their life. You could be gung-ho and ready to chat, but if you can tell the other person is closed off, uncomfortable, or acting in a way that doesn't feel inviting, this might not be the right time to start a conversation with this particular person.

4. Volley your experiences and thoughts back and forth to generate momentum on a topic once you've got the ball rolling. Here's the thing, try not to get so excited and worked up that you word-vomit everything you're thinking and feeling at them all at once. Sloooow and steady wins this race.

5. If someone asks a question you're comfortable answering, give an in-depth, meaningful response. You could even end your bit with a question for them if you want to continue the forward momentum.

6. Do not ever feel like you owe anyone your energy who you feel genuinely uncomfortable

around. Read each situation to see if the person is kind towards you. Most cases are friendly, but even good conversations can sometimes feel awkward. Just remember that if you feel nervous, the other person will likely feel anxious too. So please treat them with kindness and expect kindness in return. Otherwise, exit the situation.

7. It doesn't need to be weird when you're ready to end a conversation that seems like it might never end. You can say, "I had an awesome time talking to you! Unfortunately, I must go now, but we can catch up soon."

Making friends and learning how to communicate is multifaceted, to say the least. The most important thing is to be authentic. When you branch into new experiences and meet people who share common interests, strengths, and hobbies, it will become easier to make new friends. Remember that small gestures of kindness also count, not just what you give to others but also what they extend to you in return. All relationships require balance, an equal give and take between two parties. Show up for your people, and your people will show up for you.

TABLE MANNERS AND GOOD PUBLIC BEHAVIOR.

I'm not saying family pizza night wearing your pajamas, elbows on the table, and licking the grease rolling down your forearms has to go! Not at all, and actually, I just laughed at the image I now have in my head. I'm saying that maybe don't do that when family pizza night ends up being at a local Italian restaurant with your sibling's girlfriend and your dad's new boss as your company. (shrugs) It is what it is. We tame those wild, comfy animal instincts to show respect for others by being considerate and polite. And as cozy as you might feel slurping down a plate of spaghetti, I don't judge I do it too; it might not be appetizing for the other people who are also trying to enjoy their meal. But before I end up talking about every horribly embarrassing dinner outing my kids put me through, here's a good place to get started when learning the "dos" and "don'ts" of the restaurant industry.

1. When the waiter arrives, remember that they're human beings with feelings and a life. So be polite and greet them. They may want to tell you about the specials for that day, so listen and give them your attention.

2. Dress appropriately for the occasion. Prom and other school dances come with their own set of rules and attire, but in general, each restaurant or public outing with have a stipulated expectation for dress code. If you aren't sure what to wear, you can check their website or ask your parents.

3. Posture! Yes, it counts. Sitting up straight and keeping your elbows off the table is a must. When you slouch or keep your head down, it implies you're bored and shows disrespect to the people spending time with you. It's especially rude if they're paying for your meal.

4. When you sit at the table, one of the first things you can do is put the napkin in your lap.

5. If you have a retainer, remove it before sitting at the table. Period. If you forgot to take it out before you sat down, excuse yourself from the table and remove it privately in the restroom.

6. Please, I beg you, please do NOT put your chewing gum under the table or on the edge of your plate. Instead, you can wrap it in a disposable napkin. Otherwise, chuck it in the trash before you sit down.

7. Wait until everyone is served before you begin unless the table host announces that they'd like you to start.

8. Chew with your mouth closed. That's it. No elaboration. Just close your mouth.

9. Try not to make noises while you eat. The sounds of chewing loudly and slurping don't tend to appeal to the appetites of others.

10. When you're sitting at the dinner table, grooming yourself, such as applying makeup or brushing your hair, can send microscopic – and sometimes not so microscopic – skin and hair particles into the air, which land in everyone's food. So preen and primp in appropriate areas, the dinner table not being one.

11. When you finish your meal, place your knife and fork on the side of the plate next to each other. This gesture signals to the wait staff that you finished your meal, and they are free to remove the dish from in front of you.

Please feel free to follow these tips as a guideline for most American-based restaurants. Remember that different cultures and religions have their unique traditions and rules. Respect your beliefs and always do your best.

HOW AND WHEN TO LEAVE A TIP.

Here's a good place for a segue from the previous points about restaurants to roll into a discussion about tipping. One common misconception is the belief that servers get paid a regular hourly wage, but this is not true. Most wait staff get paid an hourly rate between $2 and $4 per hour because they greatly rely on receiving tips for their service. To help you better understand what to expect, I will break down a list of questions and answers about tipping in restaurants and other service providers.

1. Tipping at restaurants and coffee shops should be 18-20% after the sales tax. If the bill doesn't automatically show you the tip amount to add for 18-20%, here is a fast way to use your cell phone calculator to do the math. If your bill total after tax is $14.76, and you want to leave a 20% tip, pull up your calculator and type: 14.75x 0.20 = 2.95. Your tip amount is $2.95. Now, add that to the total$14.75 + $2.95 = $17.70 is your TOTAL after tip.

2. If you're dining in a large group – 9 people total, including yourself – and you all agree to split the tip based on the bill's total, here's how you calculate that amount. Say the bill total

after tax is $126.92 and you all agree to a tip of %18. Use your calculator and type: 126.92 x 0.18 = 22.85 The total tip amount is $22.85. Let's split it nine ways. On your calculator: 22.85 ÷ 9 = 2.54. The tip per person is $2.54. Add that amount to the total portion of your bill. *Note that if you all decide to split the bill 9 ways, add the tip amount to the total bill and then divide by the number in your party. *

3. If you tip a taxi/ride share or food delivery person, 10-15% of the total cost is appropriate.
4. Many people don't realize that tipping is expected in nail, hair, and massage establishments. The normal tip amount is 18-20%, like that in a restaurant.

Tipping is appropriate when you're responsible for paying for the service provided to you. There are times when tipping would therefore be considered inappropriate, so here are several people for whom it is not necessary to tip: Teachers, medical professionals, employees, package-delivery people, sports coaches, camp counselors, or school bus drivers.

Other common questions regarding tipping can sometimes arise from awkward situations. Like, what if you genuinely were not satisfied with your service? Or should you tip if you don't have extra money? There's a simple answer to both understandable questions.

You should always tip no matter what.

If the service you received was unsatisfactory, then it's time you put your new-found communication skills to use and speak with a manager. Calmly describe the situation, but never, ever, stiff the server. For example, if you have a part-time job someday and do less than satisfactory work, your boss doesn't keep your paycheck from you. Instead, they would pull you aside and have a professional conversation to correct the problem.

If you find yourself in the other scenario where you don't have enough money to leave a tip, you may want to find a different restaurant that is more affordable. However, no server should work for free, so an alternative meal source might be necessary if you cannot afford to tip.

BASIC MANNERS FOR EVERY TEEN.

If you have memories flashing before your eyes of your parents telling you to tuck in your shirt, get off your cell phone, spend time with your family, and remind you to say "please" and "thank you," then this section is here to help. I get it. It doesn't make you feel great to get constantly reminded to mind your manners. But I do want to remind you that you're the one who wants to gain independence and grow up wisely. Using good manners doesn't just show your parents respect, but you'll earn it for yourself in return. So let's go over some manners you'll take with you and use everywhere from now on.

1. Say "please" and thank you." If you want something, remember you aren't entitled to it, and therefore you are requesting it by saying "please." Likewise if you receive something from someone, say "thank you" for their efforts.

2. Take accountability and offer a sincere apology when you've done something that warrants one. An example is, "I'm sorry I hurt your feelings. I should have considered how that would make you feel." Here is an example that sounds like an apology but is not: "I'm sorry you feel that way. I didn't mean to hurt your feelings." See the difference? Take accountability and grow from it. If someone feels bad about something you did or said, it isn't up to you to decide how they are supposed to feel. Own it like a grown-up and give a genuine apology.

3. A real mature move is to ask a question or for help when you need it. Of course, you don't

know what you don't know, and it doesn't make you stupid. But, unfortunately, there's a lot of information in this big ol' world, and there's no possible way for you – or anyone for that matter – to have an answer for everything.

4. Ask permission!! This can go hand in hand with #3 above because it takes a big person to admit they don't know everything. In this instance, asking permission shows respect for boundaries and will keep you out of a lot of potential trouble.

5. Unless it is an emergency, do NOT answer texts, alerts, or calls when talking face-to-face with another person. Other places to avoid cell phones: School, at work clocked in, on a date, during an interview, while you're spending quality time with someone, at the movies (I will personally toss you out of the theatre myself lol), at a restaurant, or anywhere that doesn't allow the use of them.

6. Say "excuse me" to get someone's attention or after you burp.

7. Wait your turn to speak in a conversation, and don't grab things from them or touch other people.

Having good manners does take practice. As you morph into a young adult after leaving your childhood cocoon, you'll need to practice mindfulness of these manners and habits. When you were a child, you were oblivious to others and lacked the self-control and discipline it takes to call yourself mature. Over time, these manners become habits; once they form, you'll not even notice you're doing them. You won't think twice about standing for an older man so he can sit on the crowded subway or hold the door for others. It will become a part of who you are and a beautiful part indeed.

DATING ADVICE.

One of the most fun yet nerve-racking experiences to look forward to as a teenager is dating! We talked earlier about wanting to fit in and avoid rejection, and it's no secret that dating can lead you to feel exceptionally jittery when you have a crush on someone. The prospect of messing up could scare you off the hunt entirely. But don't let it! We'll get you there. Hopefully, these will help you gain a lot of confidence when you're not sure where to start.

1. Try not to rush into dating if you don't feel ready. There's a massive difference between

feeling emotionally stable and wanting to date vs. you feel like everyone else is dating, so you should also. You know yourself better than any other person alive, so don't let your peers dictate what's best for you. What's more, you're likely to end up rushing into a relationship that might not be healthy or satisfying if it isn't something you want to do. You could also hurt the other person, and that is not OK.

2. Listen and trust your intuition. It's there for a reason, and you will know the difference between nervous excitement and the anxiety of something feeling wrong.

3. Respect boundaries! Ask, ask, ask. No means no; if they say yes, double or triple-check. And no, I'm not being extra.

4. Being confident is awesome, but being cocky and disrespecting someone is not. Everything loops back to good communication. Be truthful and ask for the truth in return.

5. Clearly define your relationship. If you want to be exclusive, but your crush does not, then this relationship will not work for either of you.

6. A good relationship happens when both parties are whole themselves all on their own. Meaning they each have their own identities and lives

and don't want or need validation from others to hold them up and make them feel complete.

7. Earn respect by showing respect. Period.

Love, Lust, or Infatuation.

At this period in your life, while you're sexually maturing and hormones are going bananas, it's going to be hard to tell the difference between these three: Love, lust, and infatuation.

Love is deep and compassionate. You want the best for the other person, even if that excludes you from the picture. Lust is often confused for love because it is such an intense sexual desire, but it is not long-lasting and does not consider the other person's feelings. Infatuation doesn't have to be sexual, but it is intense. It's usually short-lived passion or admiration for another person, but if left unchecked, it breeds obsession. If you aren't sure what you're feeling, I urge you to speak with a school counselor or an adult you trust.

Relationship Abuse.

Abuse. We don't suspect it when we go into something wanting love, vulnerability, honesty, and commitment. But unfortunately, abuse does happen, and it happens to those of us who want to love the most. I'm asking you not to skip this section because abuse is often disguised in covert forms. So, I will cover several ugly forms of abuse to be aware of and how to keep yourself safe.

Different forms of abuse include physical, sexual, financial, digital, and stalking. All of these are different, yet they all have the same basis. Abuse is repeated misuse with a sinister purpose or intent. If you confront an abuser, they will likely tell you you're mistaken, you're exaggerating, or they may even tell you that you deserve it. You must protect and love yourself more than you love anyone else. This is important and necessary. It is not selfish: It's self-love and compassion. And when you love yourself, you'll listen to your intuition and set good boundaries, so these nasty kinds of people won't be allowed back in your life. Other warning signs you're in a relationship include but are not limited to:

1. Your partner consistently puts you down and makes you feel bad.
2. Isolates you from friends and family.
3. Checks your phone for messages and calls from other people.
4. Uses social media accounts to watch with whom you interact.
5. Makes you feel helpless or weak if you try to leave them.
6. Threatens you in any way.

7. Forces you into decisions with which you're uncomfortable.
8. Makes you feel guilty.
9. Hurts you physically, emotionally, or mentally.

I need to make this clear to you: You are important. You are significant. You matter. Take care of yourself first! If something doesn't feel right, no one gets to tell you how you're supposed to feel. Do not talk yourself out of your intuition or feelings because they're there to protect you. Listen to them and get yourself help! Stand in your truth, not theirs. They're going to confuse you, and I deeply understand how painful this can be. But you're going to get help, and in the future, you're going to avoid these situations because you're going to learn from them.

Make Yourself Safe!

These are just a couple of ideas to help keep you safe from predators, and yes, this goes for everyone.

1. Have a curfew you work out with your parents.
2. Let your parents meet your date. Adults have had time to sharpen their spidey senses, so sniffing they might help to sniff out the bad apples. Please keep them in the loop with where you're going and with whom.

3. Go on group dates! It's fun, too.
4. Meet in a public place.
5. Don't send nudes or sexts. I'm not saying this to be an old prude; I'm telling you this because you shouldn't send anything out that you wouldn't want everyone in the world to see. So please take my word for it and don't test this yourself.
6. Get drinks yourself! Keep track of your drinks. It's that simple. Drugging and date rape is real!! It's not a joke, and I'm not playing.

We've covered dating, abuse, and keeping yourself safe. There are so many scenarios in the world, but this will cover the basics. I want to convey this message: Protect yourself while you explore your new life. Meet new people and go on dates! Enjoy this time in your life before full-fledged adulthood. I'm just asking you to love yourself and trust yourself first. If you ever need help, ask your parents -or an adult you trust- for it without hesitation. Now we can move into how to handle yourself in the online world of social entertainment and dating with: *Staying Safe Online*.

STAYING SAFE ONLINE

"Don't say anything online that you wouldn't want plastered on a billboard with your face on it."

— ERIN BURY

I'm sure you know that your family truly wants the best for you. But so that you can hear it again, *They genuinely want what's best for you.* But, as cliché as it may be, you won't fully understand their love for you until you're an adult, possibly with your own kids to raise. I'm bringing this up because you need to see their – and my- perspective on the online world. I promise they aren't trying to be controlling, domineering parents who don't understand you. They aren't trying to keep you from learning and exploring. They have, however, experienced some of the horrors this world has to offer. They understand what people are capable of, and with the internet being so freely at your fingertips, it's a whole new world from which they are tasked with protecting you. Ha! And they thought raising kids in the real world was challenging.

I've shared some bullet-point ideas about how and why you need to keep yourself safe online.

INTERNET STATISTICS ON SAFETY.

1. Every 39 seconds, an internet attack occurs.
2. Internet-based harassment has affected 12% of users.
3. Teens are susceptible targets of cyberbullying or threats of violence, coming in at over 59%.
4. 1 in 7 minors is contacted online by someone with sexual intentions.
5. Minors likely view pornographic content by the age of 15.
6. If you're doing something online, you wouldn't want your parents to find out; you're likely doing something that could cause harm to yourself, even if you don't know it.

7. If an older person wants to talk to your or be your friend or send sexual messages to you, this is a predator. If a stranger wants to meet you somewhere, this is a predator. If someone is trying to get you to send them pictures or money, this is a scammer. I don't care how nice they seem. You cannot trust this person, and you must tell an adult or authority figure immediately. Not just for your safety but for protecting other teens and younger kids who this person could target and hurt. Now is a good time to be a hero and save lives by turning these creeps in to the police.

8. Bullying can, has, and will kill teens. It would help if you had this discussion with your parents because it's a serious topic. 85% of teens experience online bullying because it's easy for bullies to hide behind screens. Don't be a bully, and don't put yourself in a position to get bullied.

There's a BIG difference between growing into adulthood and imitating adult-like behavior online, where you can pretend to feel older or more mature. So don't confuse those two things.

INTERNET RISKS AND SAFETY.

1. Pornography and violence -actual or simulated- in movies, shows, or games. I get it, you're a teenager who's developing sexually. That isn't bad, and no shame shall come your way. But you might not realize the long-term effects this content can have on your brain during development. Both pornography and violence create neuropathways in your brain that can alter the way you view yourself, your relationships, other humans, and your environment in very negative ways.

2. Hate sites and terrorist sites. If you don't like stereotypes, cruelty, or bullying directed at you, don't you dare turn that around on other people. Please don't be a human with the potential to be and do good, but instead allow hatred to infiltrate their minds and hearts. You're bigger than that.

3. Fake news! Ugh, I can't deal with fake news. It gets me sometimes, too. It looks real! So, my advice is to check to see if it's a reputable source before you believe it. P.S.- No, the Onion is not a real news outlet.

4. If your goal is to be happy while alive, don't look for sites encouraging the use of drugs,

alcohol, self-harm, or suicide. On the other hand, feeling depressed isn't to be shrugged off. I've noticed teens who were massively depressed but didn't know what to do or whom to tell. If you aren't comfortable talking to a parent or adult authority figure, please contact the suicide and crisis prevention hotline by dialing 988 or visiting www. wannatalkaboutit.com.

5. You're not getting coddled on this one; sorry about it: if you send nude pictures of yourself over the internet or via text, they have the potential for distribution throughout the world wide web. It's facts, fam.

6. Sexting. This is extremely dangerous. I'm not talking about how impolite it is to be immodest. I'm talking about how people can share the context of your messages for money and find ways to rope you into human sex trafficking. If someone hints at this kind of communication, please do yourself a favor and report them. So, what if someone you know or even have a crush on asks for a sext? Well, you might want to. But it doesn't remove the danger of publicly having that information leaked. So, if you're going to participate, please, at the very least, don't send naked pictures. If they push you for

it, they aren't respecting you or your boundaries, and this is not a high honor. (Slow waves goodbye to the person you thought they were). There's always the possibility that if you send texts or images you regret, here's what I want you to do first: Take a deep breath with your eyes closed and notice how you're alive and well. This, too, shall pass. Let a trusted adult know what happened, but not a peer, if you can avoid it. If an image gets leaked online and you're under 18 years of age, you must immediately contact the police. Untag yourself from the photo. Report the image. Report the person who posted it. Tell a teacher if that person goes to your school. And last but not least, don't you dare beat yourself up for this. You're already learning a hard lesson, but you'll make it through this. Next, you need to talk to a therapist or a counselor to process what's happened. You have people who love you; this is precisely the time to lean on your support system.

7. Make sure each password you use is different from website to website. Never store your information in your phone or give details of your accounts to anyone other than your parents. The longer the password and more

characters, the harder it is to hack. One type of scam involves stealing your online banking information to make unauthorized purchases.

8. Do you still want to grow up and prove yourself to the world? Learn to regulate your habits by setting your online time limits. You know you have other things to do, so assess a timeframe that works in your schedule and let your parents check it out. I guarantee they'll look at you wide-eyed, both eyebrows arched way up, and the corner of their mouth might turn up in a quirk of a smile. The point is, every opportunity you get to show them that you're growing, do it. (Hands you bonus points)

9. Identity theft probably doesn't register much on your radar, which is why it should. Hackers and scammers know this isn't at the forefront of your mind, and there are some creative ways to steal your personal information via technology these days. The big takeaway for you is to know that once someone steals your identity, it can follow you for the rest of your life. If your credit is destroyed, buying a house, getting a car, and using a credit card might be tricky. Keep track of your electronic devices and fitness trackers, and don't divulge your information willingly to apps you're

downloading. Research each app before you use it. Protect yourself!

OK, now that I've hammered a lot of the hard stuff, I'll briefly touch on a few basics for you to talk to your parents about if you have questions.

EMAIL BASICS

- Don't open or click on suspicious links in emails or web pages.
- Don't reply to emails from banks, credit unions, loan officers, etc.
- If something looks suspicious, don't open it to find out. Instead, please send it to spam. The company will contact your phone or send a follow-up email if it's a legitimate email.
- It sounds obvious, but don't disclose personal information over the phone or online.

SCAMS

- Online shopping is fantastic! Just make sure it's an actual store before you buy something. Check reviews and ask friends or family if they've heard of the website.

- Free public Wi-Fi is unsecured, so it's easier for hackers to access your information. Consider using a VPN while in public.
- Everything you post is permanent and can be used against you.
- Online friends should be your well-known, in-person friends only. Don't accept friend requests from strangers. Besides, you should think of yourself as exclusive. You don't need everyone to have access to you.

GOOD INTERNET HABITS TO FORM

- Don't say anything online that wouldn't get you accepted into college, a job, or an internship. The first thing companies do when they get your application is google your name.
- Ask permission from others before you post their pictures or tag them.
- Humor is great! Use it! But if it's coming from a bad place, you might be using passive aggression, which isn't cool. So check yourself before you wreck yourself.
- Exercise caution when talking about religion or politics. Remember that your opinions are just that; opinions. Be respectful of the opinions

and beliefs of others just as you wish them to be to you.

- You hold a lot of power in your ability to access and use the internet. So be a wise leader and control yourself while accessing this binary world of unlimited information.

As a parent, I can say this with conviction; if something happens online that makes you feel wrong, you will be supported and praised for being brave enough to come to us with these issues. Parents know this online world exists, and we want you to be ready. And if something happens, we want you to know that we love you and have your back no matter what.

Now that we've covered the importance of protecting yourself and others online, let's look at getting you some life experience and your own money in chapter 5: *Getting Your First Job.*

5

GETTING YOUR FIRST JOB

8

"Opportunities don't happen, you create them."

— CHRIS GROSSER.

Congratulations!! Making it to this chapter means you've begun the inner work towards maturing, getting you that much closer to your goal of independence. Of course, the idea of your first job will elicit excitement and apprehension, which is normal and expected. While you're stoked to have money in your pocket, like all new things, it can be a daunting first step. Without a lot of life experience under your belt, figuring out what the right job is for you might feel like a mountain. But once you read ahead and follow the steps I've laid out for you, most of the pressure should be removed, and you'll have a clear view of forging ahead.

FINDING THE JOB THAT WORKS FOR YOU!

We're about to dive into your passions and time frames, but first, let's look at your current academic standing. Before you make moves to get a job, which is beneficial but takes up time, do you have the grades you need to graduate? And maybe you don't want only to graduate high school, but you want to make sure you can get into college or any other academic level with GPA requirements. If you're not where you need to be to succeed in the future, then a job can wait. But remember, you'll be working most of your life, so it's more important to bump up those grades to set you up for comfort later.

Ok, let's get started!

Job Categories for Teens. https://www.indeed.com/career-advice/finding-a-job/how-to-find-job-as-teenager

1. Part-time is a job where you can work after school or on the weekends. A full-time position

    is 40 hours a week, which you will not have time for while in school.

2. Contract jobs are short-term jobs, usually several weeks in length. Construction jobs, for example, often contract because they're on a set amount of time to finish a project. The job concludes once the project is complete.

3. Seasonal work is popular with teens because while on summer break, you can work full-time at a local swimming pool or as a camp counselor.

4. Internships are usually unpaid positions suitable for teens looking to work in the medical field. Although they do not pay, many companies can offer school credit.

5. If you're considering owning a business as an entrepreneur, then part-time jobs like babysitting, dog walking, house cleaning, or tutoring might be a good place to start. However, serving is also a great way to learn to be your own boss because the amount and quality of work you provide are directly proportional to the amount of money brought in.

There are many different types of jobs, but I gave you a few to get your feet wet. The most important part of this process is deciding what kind of job will suit your personality best. I bet you can look back a year and see how much you've changed in that short time. Now imagine how different you'll be a year from now! The point I'm making here is that this job is meant to fit who you are at this moment. Your goal is to earn money, learn transferable skills from one job to the next, evaluate what you like and dislike in a workplace, and grow your emotional IQ to make you a better person and future job candidate.

When deciding where you'd like to apply, first set some limits for yourself. These should include rests/break needs, meals, employment certifications (if applicable), and minimum hourly wages for tipped and non-tipped employees. It's also a necessary plan to figure out the logistics of getting to and from your job. If you're not old enough to drive, you'll need a reliable source of transportation like a bike or a family member who is committed to getting you there on time. The distance to a job will also play a significant role in your decision. Another consideration is your age. The legal age for part-time employment in the United States is 14 years old, and if you're 16 years old or younger, you'll need to check your state's hourly work cap.

Okay, so let's get down to it: What job is interesting enough for you to get out of bed on a Saturday morning or immediately after school once or twice a week? Consider a few things for yourself before you jump to answering that question. What are your genuine interests and skills? I didn't randomly throw the word "genuine" in there for no reason. I did it because I know the temptation to go to work with friends or to be closer to someone you're crushing on. First, remember that you're doing this to step out of your comfort zone to grow. Teens who pair up to stay comfortable miss the chance to meet new people and learn to stand on their own. Plus, having too much fun and getting into trouble is easy. I know this all too well. (smirks) On the other hand, working any job that doesn't fit you well will feel like a miserable life sentence, even if you're only there once or twice a week.

DEVELOP YOUR SKILLS.

Since we're on the subject, what skills do you want to develop? If you aren't sure where your weaknesses lie, sit down with your parents and ask them for guidance. Learning to use a company computer and software is a great skill. But what about building personality skills, such as communicating clearly to build confidence? For example, if you're shy because you don't feel strong talking to strangers, taking a job as a barista at a coffee shop might be a great idea. There are minimal, transient interactions with customers where no personal information is exchanged between you. You'll learn a script to handle the transaction, a drinks list, and how to cash someone out. After some time, you'll have gotten used to looking people in the face and interacting with them. You'll learn that you can be charming and kind, and after you're more comfortable, you may even improvise on what to say as guests arrive. These are precisely the kinds of experiences I want you to have. I know they're awkward and scary initially, but it's only to help you become the best version of yourself.

PINPOINT YOUR EXISTING INTERESTS AND SKILLS.

Don't be shy! You know you have unique talents and interests just waiting for you to unlock their potential. It might be a good plan to sit down and write about your strengths so you can take your time and focus. Sometimes we feel timid to admit our greatness for fear of sounding too proud or getting rejected. When you're writing this down in private, the only person who can reject these claims is you, and you aren't going to do that. If you write for yourself, you're not only affirming these strengths but are more likely to bring them to fruition. Here are several strengths to think about that you might not even realize you have.

- Cleverness. You come up with unique, out-of-the-box solutions or answers.
- Humorous. You make people laugh, which is the best medicine.
- Kindness. Caring for others on a deep and passionate level heals you and others.
- Intelligence. That brain of yours holds a wealth of knowledge, so use it!
- Spontaneous. The adventurer in you seeks new experiences, which builds character.
- Companionship. Others feel safe in your presence because you seek not to harm.
- Stamina. Your hard work shows a level of endurance to back it up.
- Charisma. You are putting people at ease with your lack of judgment, and you show clever wit.
- Organized. You know where everything is, and you have an outline in your mind to make use of efficiency.

Interests vary from person to person, and it's meant to be that way. If we were all the same, imagine how dull life would be. So, what sparks your imagination and brings out these strengths in you?

Think of something that brings you a lot of joy. Maybe you imagine baking gingerbread men's cookies during the holiday season with your family. You remember the smells of the sugary treats, the oven's heat keeping you warm from the cold of the snow outside. Cheerful movies play on TV while everyone is wrapped in blankets on the couch, and the lights feel magical. Since then, you've loved helping bake brownies or cupcakes for birthday parties. You're the first to volunteer to roll out the dough for pastries. It might not have occurred to you that baking is a skill you have. Why not use it? That way, when Saturday morning rolls around, and you hop out of bed to start a new job, it's heading into a bakery to do what you love and do best.

Interests and skills often develop from life experiences we might think of when tapping into our psyche to discover ourselves. For example, I've always had a knack for working with people, so when starting a part-time job in high school, I chose businesses that encouraged person-to-person interaction. I'd even worked my way as a grocery store clerk, to a stock person, and eventually into the position of Dairy Manager. It was good money, and I was good at it. It ultimately led me to the career I've cultivated for 36 years in reality, and I've proudly done very well for myself and in supporting a growing family.

Once you've dug deep and decided on a few plausible job ideas, it's time to start hunting for the places in your area looking to hire for those positions.

HAPPY JOB HUNTING!

1. Now that you've learned to navigate the internet safely, jumping online to Indeed.com, your local newspaper or specific businesses you're interested in will have recent job listings for which you can apply.

2. Newspapers! Ha! Ok, look. Don't make fun of me for loving an old-school newspaper. They're one of the simple pleasures in life. To open a newspaper at the kitchen table in a bathrobe with some coffee before the rest of the house is awake is sublime. Anyhow, back to job hunting. Yes! Even newspapers are great resources for finding locally advertised jobs. Newspaper companies know that there are people like you trying to find a suitable workplace, so there's a "Hiring" section in everyone I've seen.

3. Walking by local business storefronts is a great place to find a job close to your home. If you can walk to a storefront, you know you can work there without the need for an external source of transportation.

4. Word of mouth is one of the best ways to get a job anywhere. Many jobs don't even advertise because they entirely rely on their employees to ask their friends or family if they'd like a position with the company. This is also another way to get more comfortable striking up conversations with people. Still don't feel confident to walk up and start talking? Asking if they know of a job that's hiring is a terrific way to get a friend AND get a job. It's not weird at all, I promise.

ACE YOUR APPLICATION.

Hey, look at you! Well done on finding a workplace and team you want to join! The next step is to research your state's laws requiring work permits for teenagers. For example, in Florida, you do not need a work permit, but you do need to show legal documentation of your identifying information, such as your name and age.

As you prepare a resume, there are a few things to consider. First, you can't just walk into the job and say, "Hey, give me a job!" Actually, I guess you could do that, but I'd imagine you'd be unsuccessful in obtaining employment. If you want to work somewhere to make money, you'll need to show them why it would benefit them to hire you. Wanting a job is excellent, but now you're going to make them like you to work for them. Remember earlier when I said there are amazing things about yourself that you should write down? That's going to come in handy. Without previous employment, you want to show your academic achievements and extracurricular and personal successes. So while you'll organize your thoughts on how you'd like to present yourself, here's a quick breakdown of some basic information you'll provide on your resume.

KEY SECTIONS OF A RESUME.

- Contact information. This should be your name, phone number, email address, and city/state.
- Professional Summary. If you don't have a previous work history, that's ok. Here's where you can talk about special recognition and awards at school, valuable talents, or a summary of why you're excited to work at this establishment.
- Education. Pretty clear-cut. Disclose what grade you're currently attending, and if you have an excellent attendance record, mention that as well. Showing you take school seriously tells an employer that you're responsible enough to take a job seriously.

- Skills! You can do many things well, but you might not realize it would benefit a company. For example, are you good at using a computer or technology? That's a skill. Are you good at typing words quickly? That's a skill. Can you send an email and use WordDocs? That's a skill. Are you able to make the change from a $20 bill? That's a skill. Are you artistic or creative? That's a talent. Can you build things with your hands? That's a talent. Do you see where I'm going with this? You're full of valuable skills. Please don't be shy. Go ahead and mention them. Calling attention to your strength sends the message to the hiring manager that you know your worth and that you have a high value.

HOW TO MAKE A RESUME.

Before you begin, go back to the job description, and read it thoroughly. There are tiny details that may be easy to miss, and you want to get a complete picture of what they expect from you as an employee. You also want to know what to expect from them as your employer. This information will help you tailor the resume to fit the job.

1. You first want an employer to notice your name and contact information. It should be bold, enlarged, and stand out at the page's very top.

2. I mentioned that you should include a professional summary, but a personal summary is excellent, too, especially if you don't have prior work experience. Then, after looking over the details of the job description, think about the skills you have that would make you a good fit for that job.

For example, pretend you're applying for a job cleaning and detailing cars at a local dealership. The job requires a valid state ID and a minimum of 15 years old. They expect a turn-over-time of 30 minutes per car in an 8-hour day and a minimum of 12 vehicles detailed by the end of the shift. Take a minute to examine the abilities you'd need to succeed in this job. You'd want to be efficient and organized to clean the cars as they'd train you. Some physical exertion, bending, squatting, and moderate lifting would occur. And you'd need to be very diligent in keeping track of your time, so you'd want to have a reliable watch with a timer.

If you scoured the job description and said to yourself, "Yep! This is for me!" then it's time you look at some experiences where you've used those same skills so you can expound upon them on your resume. You might say that you've helped your dad fix cars since you were a kid, and include some specifics to show you have a passion for cars and the ability to do some physical work. If you've woken up to your alarm every morning and never missed school due to running late, that's a great way to show accountability for time. Voilà!

If you have work experience, then you'll add that below your education information.

3. When you write your statement, you won't do a great job selling your best qualities by using dull, lazy, boring, unmotivated, or tired adjectives. You wouldn't want to hire someone heavy in those dreary qualities, and neither do they. Besides, you're doing your daily affirmations, and you know you're an incredible human. So, use the adjective which you embody to entice the manager to pick up their phone and offer you an interview. When describing yourself, here are a few strong, positive adjectives to use:

- Self-motivated. You've gotta be! They expect you to work when you start a job, not wait around to find something to do.
- Dedicated. Put your mind to the task and complete it to the best of your abilities.
- Energetic. Body language and personality combined will tell a whole story. But let that story be one of vigor and optimism.

- People-oriented. Make a conscious effort to treat your co-workers with kindness and respect. Show respect to earn respect.

4. Now's the time to show off any academic achievements or awards you've won! It's also wise to include any relevant classes you've taken or extracurricular activities/hobbies/interests relating to the job you're applying for.

5. Highlight any volunteer experience you've had. It might not be a "job," but it's organized hard work, and a boss will respect the effort.

6. Include ALL extracurricular activities. Are you in a bowling club? Great, add it. Do you babysit for the neighbors occasionally? Put it on there. ANY and ALL experiences where you've had to use logic, independence, and discernment will set you apart from the crowd.

7. Leadership is also a great resume booster. You don't have to be the student council president to claim leadership. For example, have you ever been in a group project where you took charge and delegated tasks to others? Or offered to assist a teacher in classroom duties? These are leadership skills you're using and maybe didn't realize it.

8. Let's hear it if you have personal projects outside of school or groups! For example, are you a creative writer for your weekly dungeons and dragons meetings, or do you build wooden bird boxes for your backyard? These might feel like fun past times to you, but they show others that you take the initiative to expand your horizons and aren't a mindless zombie glued to the television 24/7.

I can't stress this enough: PROOFREAD YOUR RESUME! Even 1, 2, and 3 times. It would be best to get it right rather than turn it in with spelling or grammatical errors and not get a call back because you were sloppy. I also recommend using professional websites such as Indeed.com to give you some resume template ideas. It'll make the process much faster and give you a good visual guide.

Resume Writing Tips.

1. Stick to a professional font style like Times New Roman, Calibri, or Arial. As fun as Apple Chancery might look, type a letter to a friend with that font, but not to an employer. They want the meat and potatoes of who you are, and simple things like inappropriate font can take away from what they're looking for. The same goes for format. There are a lot of cool designs for resumes available to you, but sticking with a classic format gets the important points across faster than if an

employer must jump around a resume page to find the info.

2. Write your resume in chronological order because it'll be the easiest to write and it'll be the most effortless to read.

- Name and contact information.
- Summary/personal or professional statement. In a few sentences, state why you want the job and are a good candidate for the position. Make sure to highlight your best qualities.
- Education. Include the current grade you're in with your expected graduation date. You may want to add plans for college, such as your degree and college of choice. You'll also list any courses you've completed that are relevant to the job.
- Experiences. If you don't have a work history, add the beneficial life experiences I mentioned. For example, volunteering or other achievements can be listed.
- Skills! Go back and look at the list you made for yourself. Add some of the best and most relevant skills to the resume.
- Honors and achievements.

- Hobbies and interests. This is optional, of course, but if you have something you want to share, then go ahead!

3. Keep your resume to ONE page.

4. Save your document under PDF, so it's easy to email and upload to online job applications.

5. If you don't have a professional email set up, do that before you add your contact information. SoccerGuuu-uuurl08@email.com or CODSniperGuy@email.com are inappropriate emails when communicating with an employer, college, business, or professional person. Make an email with your name in it if possible. Good examples are Damion.Brown1@email.com or Lilly MHansborough44@email.com

WHEN AND WHY TO ADD A COVER LETTER.

Cover letters are a one-page introduction of yourself to an employer. Yes, you're still going to write a resume listing your qualifications. But this is a nice way to show the person hiring for a position that you know the job and want it. A cover letter is meant to catch their attention when there are multiple candidates for a job, and you want to stand out. This will encourage the manager to read your resume. Then, you'll mention a few of your skills and experiences that match the job you're applying for and end the cover letter positively by requesting an interview or meeting.

Different Types of Cover Letters.

Remember that cover letters are unique and different for each job you apply for. You'll address the hiring manager or person reading your resume by their name, such as 'Mr.' or 'Ms.' Followed by their last name. Try not to begin a cover letter generically with "To Whom it May Concern." Addressing them by their name shows you care enough to put in the effort to customize this to them, and it isn't a stock cover letter you sent to everyone else.

Pro tip: If the hiring manager's name isn't in the job posting, you need to call and ask for their name.

As with resume writing, there are excellent cover letter examples and templates online to learn from. Your situation is unique, so you'll look for a template that best matches your circumstance. Here are a few cases to consider and research when writing your own.

- Not having work experience.
- Having minimal work experience.

- If you're applying for a position that isn't advertised, but you want to work for a company.
- Cover letters should still be appropriately formatted and sent, even if the job doesn't require a resume.

Here's What to Include in Your Cover Letter.

1. Your contact information. It won't be as bold and upfront as on your resume. This will be on the lefthand margin, like that when writing a letter.
2. The contact information of the person you're addressing in the cover letter. Their name, position at the company, and contact details.
3. The title of the position.
4. A FEW skills relevant to the job written in summary describing your qualification for the position. Remember, if you're also sending a resume with your skills listed, it'll be redundant to add all of them to a short cover letter.
5. At the end, ask them to contact you to set up a good time for an interview.

Keep the cover letter brief, less than one page. You're simply summarizing your resume in a concise way that feels like you're speaking for yourself. Other things to consider during your writing process is to avoid overusing "I". Don't mention other job applications, and don't forget to hand sign or type your name at the end! You've got this.

FILLING OUT A JOB APPLICATION.

I think filling out job applications is more straightforward than building a resume if that's even an option provided by the company where you're applying. The difference between the two could be compared to a coloring book where you fill in the pre-drawn lines vs. a blank canvas with a box of oil paint where you're free to create something from scratch. The coloring book looks easier and safer because it's already laid out for you in a manner meant to look good. Just keep in mind that if you aren't careful and don't take your time, it will look a hot mess. The same goes for a job application. Don't be fooled by the fill-in-the-blank layout. This is going to require your consideration, time, and attention.

1. Take. Your. Time. Slooooow down. There's no prize for filling it out in a specific time frame. Getting it done right is what matters here.

2. Please be neat. Scout out the length of the fill-in-the-blank sections so you can choose the right size to write in. You'll always want to print your words, do not sign in cursive.

3. Answer the questions and do so honestly. You want to show you can follow directions. You also want to manage their expectations. If the job is for a Rocket Scientist -I know it isn't but just go with it for this example- don't try to make yourself sound like you're qualified for the job if you aren't. They will find out and it will be embarrassing when they fire you. You've been warned.

4. Scour your application for spelling and grammar errors. If you're filling out an application online, it's easier to correct than on a written form. If you have a written form, write all your answers and information on a separate piece of paper. Edit it before you transfer the final cut onto the application, you're turning in.

5. Be polite but formal. Employers expect reliability, punctuality, and good attendance.

6. Ask permission and gather contact information for three professional references. If you've not had a job before, you can ask to use a teacher, a volunteer coordinator, a youth group leader, or

a sports coach. These are just a few examples but try to find an adult who can speak to your work ethic and integrity. You'll need to include their names, job titles, and contact information.

7. Several days after you turn the application in, give them a follow-up call to see if they've had time to review your application. Politely ask if they'd be able to interview you -soon- for the position. Don't be pushy, be assertive.

PREPARE YOURSELF FOR AN INTERVIEW.

It's okay to be nervous, and the person interviewing you probably expects that. They've been in the same place you are now, and they'll show patience and grace as they ask you questions. Make yourself more prepared and less nervous by practicing common interview questions with family or friends before the big day.

1. "Why are you looking for a job?" -Please don't blurt out, "Because I want a paycheck!" That might be true, but they want to know why you're interested in their business. Answer honestly. Let them know if you want to develop a particular skill set, and their establishment can help.

2. "Why do you want at this company specifically?" -They already know you're interested in the field, but now they want to know what made you choose them. You need to read about the company to answer this question. Maybe you like the culture and atmosphere or know other employees who gave them a great rating.

3. "Has school prepared you for working with our company?" -Talk about those skills you've acquired! Include both academic and extracurricular successes in this discussion.

4. "Why should we hire you over other candidates?" -They know it'll take time to train you and you might be leaving them after you graduate high school. Talk about your positive qualities, like good attendance, grades, and self-discipline. Tell them if you are considering working there after high school or college.

5. "How can you become successful at this job?" -Specifically, talk about the work requirements listed in the job description and match personality traits or skill sets that complement them.

6. "Have you worked successfully on a team before?" -They don't mean work situations specifically. They're assessing if you can work

well in combination with other employees. Talk about sports teams you've played on or group science projects.

7. "What accomplishment are you most proud of?" -Think of something you worked hard to accomplish and succeeded in achieving that goal. Explain why it brought you joy and how it positively impacted your life.

8. If they ask you about salary or income expectations, you should tell them you expect pay for an entry-level or minimum-wage position. If this is a serving position or a job where you'll earn tips, they pay less per hour than regular working minimum wage.

9. "Explain a situation that was uncomfortable, but you handled it well." -Are you a problem solver or an instigator? They're trying to see how you handle conflict and the resolution to the issue. Be truthful, but make sure to pick a story that has a cheerful ending.

10. "Do your teachers or supervisors have issues or difficulty working with you?" -This might feel like a pointed question, and it sure is. However, if you start sweating because you thought of that one time in third grade your teacher caught you chasing kids on the playground with a frog, that isn't what they're asking. Do you act

with integrity and admit to your mistakes as a teenager? Even if you have less-than-10-star history, be honest about it but turn it into a learning experience you can talk about.

Items to Bring for an Interview.

- Valid ID and work papers (if needed).
- List of references.
- Completed job application, resume, and cover letter (if applicable).
- A notepad and pen.

If you feel anxious, let it be nervous excitement about a new opportunity. But remember this, too: The world does not stop spinning, and your life will continue in the right direction no matter how this interview goes. You'll practice being polite and professional and ease those nervous jitters just by expecting them to be there. Show up at least 10 minutes early, go by yourself, and be dressed appropriately. If you have questions for the interviewer, have them written in your notepad so you don't have to recall them from memory. Be grateful and thank their hand before and after the interview. Even if you don't want the job after the interview or the position goes to another candidate, send a follow-up email thanking them for their time and consideration.

Even if you bomb the interview and they don't offer you the position, this was a gift from the Universe as a trial and error to get the jitters out. You're meant to apply and interview at a different place that is better for you. Your value is not dictated by obtaining a job, so please don't feel rejected. If you get the job, this happens to be the right place at the right time. Otherwise, let's dust you off and get you back in the saddle so we can find you the tribe that attracts your vibe.

Since I've got you thinking about making money and what job's best for you, now is an excellent time to move into our next developmental area: *Money Moves to Start Now!*

6

MONEY MOVES YOU CAN NEVER START TOO EARLY

"It's not your salary that makes you rich; it's your spending habits."

— CHARLES A JAFFE.

Hey, now that you've got a new job and worked hard to earn some cash, you should treat yourself in moderation! That first paycheck you get is the first of many, and you deserve to get something that inspires and encourages you to keep going. With that being said, I don't want you to develop the self-sabotaging habit of spending every single paycheck. Keep in mind that while working part-time as a teenager, you're doing it to build up your emotional and professional backbone. At this moment in time, you aren't working to pay bills and support a family. Still, eventually, you'll need a savings account to rely on in case -God forbid- emergencies arise, and you need to use your nest egg to survive and support yourself and your family. This is where budgeting comes in. Truth be told, there's an incredible feeling of accomplishment when you budget your money and have control over your own life. Let's get started.

BUDGETING BASICS.

So, what is a budget? In simple terms, budgeting is looking at how much money (on average) you make per month and subtracting your expenses. For example, if you only make $500 per month, your expenses should never exceed that amount. When your outgoing costs exceed your incoming cash flow, it leaves you in debt. This means you owe more than you make. Next, we'll learn how to create a budget and save some dough for an emergency fund.

1. The first month you work should be when you don't spend much. You'll want to know exactly how much you can anticipate per paycheck. The basic paycheck is the base you want to rely upon when writing a budget. Bonuses, holidays, and birthday money are just that,

BONUSES! These will be excluded when deciding what money you can consistently count on. Putting this cash into savings or a rainy-day fund is best.

2. Before lavish or extraneous spending, sit down with your parents and ask them what bills you can help cover. Of course, they will likely tell you that they don't want you to pay for anything. And that's fine! But to prepare for your future bill paying as an adult by contributing $10-$50 towards your phone bill would help you mentally get the hang of budgeting around necessary expenses.

3. Keep those pay stubs! Even for online banking, having a printout in front of you will help to write down what you're earning via what you're subtracting.

4. Start collecting receipts everywhere you spend. The places you want to pay extra attention to are gas pumps and restaurants/coffee bars. If you drive or you buy gas for someone to drive you to work, this is a necessary expense you cannot avoid. Restaurants or coffee houses can be almost too fun to go to but eating out adds up FAST. Make sure you write down the tip amount you leave so you can account for every penny spent.

5. After one month of tracking your spending, analyze when you need vs. what you want. For example, if you spent your entire monthly earnings with nothing to put

into savings, you can investigate where to eliminate spending. I know it's hard, especially when it's your own money and it's so new. However, good habits can take a while to form, so I'm encouraging you to start now, so you set yourself up for success later.

6. Alright, let's look at those necessary expenses to subtract from your total earnings per month.

Let's say you've been working for three months, and you calculated an average of $700 earned per month.
Your gasoline receipts total, on average, $85 per month.
The phone bill you pay is $40 per month.
The small chunk of auto insurance you help cover is $50 per month.
That Starbucks latte you can't live without is $120 per month, tip included.
You determine these are your necessities, so these are the expenses you know you'll have no matter what.
In total: $85+$40+$50+120= $295
Round UP to be on the conservative side. ~ $300 in necessary expenses. It could be more; it could be less.
Suppose your average income is $700 - $300 = $400. That's a good amount to have left over.

7. Savings Goals with Zero-Based Budgeting! Want to know why it's so important to save money? Because when life throws unexpected situations your way, you're prepared to handle them. The general emergency fund amount is usually for 3-6 months of earnings. The good news is you don't have to save this all at once. And for now, I want you to get the hang of how to save money. It'll become more crucial when you're living independently and financially reliant upon yourself.

> If you make $700 a month and you want to save four months' worth of income, then multiply $700 x 4 = $2,800.00
> So, you want to save $2,800.00 as an emergency fund. Since we already know the amount you have left over after expenses is $400 per month, that's the value we'll be calculating from.
> Take $2,800.00 ÷ $400 = 7 months. It would take approximately seven months to save that amount of money.
> But what if you spend money on extraneous things, like going to the movies or eating out? You might have $100 left per month instead.
> We recalculate $2,800.00 ÷ $100 = 28 months or 2.33 years to save.

This is just an example, and you can adjust this amount according to your needs and lifestyle. But, again, remember this is great practice for your future!

OTHER SAVING STRATEGIES.

1. Save using the 50/30/20 rule. If you're unsure how to split your earnings for various reasons, this is a great way to divide your income. Use 50% of your earnings on essentials (such as the bills I used as an example in number 7). The 30% is used for non-essentials, and then you save 20%. This is a great way to save money faster when you aren't responsible for paying many bills yet. Remember, you can always save more if you spend less on non-essentials.
2. "Pay Yourself First." I mean, c'mon, who doesn't love how that sounds?! When you deposit that paycheck, immediately set aside a pre-determined amount into your savings account. Boom. Done. Now you can pay your bills and only spend whatever is left.
3. Envelope Budgeting. Is your new job a coffee barista or restaurant server who earns most of your income via tips? If you don't deposit the money directly into the bank, grab yourself a few envelopes. Envelope number 1: This is for

your necessities. Envelope #2: Savings.
Envelope #3: Free-spending and hobbies. For
teens, I think this is a great way to start. It
allows you to visualize your money, so if there's
none there, you can't overspend. If you have
your money in a bank account and you
overspend using a debit card, there are often
fees, and sometimes penalties charged to your
account.

4. Many banking systems let you set up a monthly
   auto-deposit from checking to savings. You will
   have control over adjusting the amount of
   money that gets auto-drafted every month.

This goes for everyone, not just teenagers, but the point
of budgeting is to spend less than you earn. Financial
advisors recommend both adults AND teenagers save
20% of their income. The tricky part is to have enough
self-control and responsibility to stick to it! Pick a day
of the month, such as the first Sunday, and analyze your
spending trends. See where you need to improve and
plan to do it.

Are you more of a visual person? I am. I like to see what
I'm working on right in front of me. You can download
a budgeting worksheet with all the categories to help
break down your expenses and keep you better on
track with your saving and spending.

Pro Tip: Every time you buy something, write it down immediately in a small notebook. This way, you consciously make purchases and aren't letting the whole "out of sight, out of mind" scenario work against you.

BUDGETING TIPS.

- Base your spending around when you get your paycheck.
- If it's too difficult to keep your spending under control while you're out with friends, that's understandable. Just do yourself a favor and leave your debit card at home. Instead, only take the amount you've allotted yourself in cash.
- It can feel good to buy things for others, but it can drain your bank account quickly. Nevertheless, you worked hard for that money, so hang onto it until you're at a place where you can comfortably pay for other people.
- Take a picture of your budgeting sheet with your phone so that you can see it anytime.

BUILDING A SAVINGS ACCOUNT.

I think I can speak for everyone who's ever opened a savings account when I say this -Depositing your first paycheck into an account and seeing the dollar amount pop up is one of the best feelings. It validates all the planning and hard work you've done to -quite literally- pay off. Just a heads up, there are a few things to know before you head off to the bank. In most states, it's illegal for any minor, a person under the age of 18 or 21 (check your state's specific requirements), to open an account without a co-signature of a parent, grandparents, or legal guardian. And yes, they check the documentation to verify you didn't ask an older sibling to pretend to be your mom.

So, here are a few types of bank accounts to research before you ask for a co-signer.

1. Regular or basic savings account. There are three different kinds that are specific for teenagers: Teen, Youth, and Student savings accounts. Your parents/co-signer can easily open an account and add your name. Easy peasy. There are usually options to remove the parent's name once you become a legal adult.

2. Custodial Accounts (UTMA) are not joint accounts. The only access the adult has to the

money in this account is whatever they deposit. You don't have access as a teenager until you become a legal adult. At that time, you're free to spend the money as you wish. It's a great way to save because you know you won't spend all of it prematurely.

3. Joint savings accounts allow you to access the money within the account at any time and will enable the adult access. Since savings accounts don't require debit cards, you will be issued an ATM card instead. You can also enroll in online banking and use safe and secure banking apps.

Pro Tip: Online savings accounts usually offer higher interest rates, so the more money you put in, the more you'll earn in interest. They typically don't have a ton of monthly maintenance fees either.

BECOME A TEEN-VESTOR!

I cannot begin to tell you how pleased you will be with yourself for starting your investing journey NOW. But unfortunately, more adults don't know how to invest their money than there are adults who do. So, I'm glad you're here so we can start your adulthood off on the right financial path.

To dangle a little carrot in front of your nose as an incentive to start investing early, here's an example of what investing for you at 15 can do for you compared to investing at 35 -according to *TheBalanceMoney*.com.

> If you deposit $150 per month into a brokerage account that gives a 10% annual return with compounding interest from the age of 15 to 60, you'd have $1.3 million dollars saved. If you started investing from 35 to 60 with these same parameters, you'd have $180,000. - *Stares at you wide-eyed, imploring you to take this seriously.*

Even if you took money out early, it would be enough to help you pay for college, travel the world, start a family, and buy a new home or a car. Be as creative as you want with it, this is your money we're talking about. I'd say that learning to save has a snowball effect: The more you save, the more you want to save. The more you want to save, the less you spend on unnecessary items; thus, you save more. And it goes round and round and round.

Without boring you with dreadful statistics, know that a significant source of anxiety and stress in most adults is due to their personal finances. Getting a nest egg started early will absolutely alleviate a lot of that worry.

Alright, but what exactly is investing? Well, you want to earn money on your earned money, right? Investing is a way to put your finances into something with the possibility of financial return or gain. It helps you save money AND gain wealth. Here's the kicker: Different types of risk are involved, depending on the investment you're interested in. I want you to make the more informed decision possible when investing, so take your looking through these and doing your research.

The HIGHS & lows of These Common Investments.

1. High-Yield Savings Account – The most basic way to begin! This is similar to a savings account but has higher interest rates, so you earn more money. However, since these are risk-free accounts, the return is low compared to other investment types.

2. Certificates of Deposit – This is an interest-earning savings account also, but you don't have access to the money at any time. These accounts require the money to be held in the account for a stipulated amount of time, often for several years. It's nice to know you have money locked away, earning interest until you're ready to open it like a great big birthday present full of cash. The FDIC insures these

accounts up to $250,000, which is also risk-free savings.

3. Stocks. – When you put your money into stocks, you become a public shareholder of a publicly traded corporation. This means you can earn dividends (a regularly paid amount of money) and capital gains (profit earned through the increase of investment). Sounds great, right?! Well, yes and no. As the stock market fluctuates drastically, so does your investment in that stock. If the company is doing well, then your investment increases. But if the company crashes, you may lose your money. That's why working for financial advisors with these investments is important. They can help point you toward the best stock investment in your price range.

4. Bonds. These are stable investments because of the financial portfolio they'll help you to build. However, they work a little differently than you might imagine. When you purchase a bond, you loan the company your money. You then receive fixed interest payments over an agreed-upon period of time.

5. Funds. Many folks like to use funds for the different securities that your money is exposed to. Funds are called "pooled investments"

because they take money from many different investors and pool it together.

- Mutual Funds pool money from multiple investors to develop a portfolio with lots of diversity. Each investor is thus part fund owner. As the fund profits, everyone profits. As it loses, everyone loses. At the end of the trading day, mutual funds get settled out.
- Exchange-Traded Funds are also pooled investments but with more securities. These trade throughout the day, like stocks, unlike the mutual fund that cashes out at the end of the day.

Opening an Investment Account for Teens.

I mentioned a type of Custodial Account known as a UTMA in the previous section, "Building a Savings Account." Still, other types of investment accounts are similar and worth mentioning.

1. A UGMA Custodial Account will hold stocks, bonds, cash, and mutual funds. The difference between this and the UTMA is that a UTMA can hold all those same assets as well as physical assets such as real estate.

2. An IRA is an individual retirement account your parents can help you set up before you're even an adult. Your family can deposit money into the account for up to a year or up to a total of $6,000.

Pro Tip: There are scams lurking around every corner in the world of investments. If it sounds too good to be true, it probably is. Always compare the promised return on investments to the rate of the market returns.

In general, it's safe to say that a high return on your investment means there will be high risk. That's different from someone promising a guaranteed but unusually high return. Don't buy into it. The same can be said about someone trying to pressure you into investing "immediately" as a "one-time exclusive offer." No. Nope. Run. You might not be a professional stock trader, but you will know enough that when an investment being offered is too difficult to understand, it's time to BAIL. (Backs away slowly)

CREATE GOOD (OR EXCELLENT) MONEY HABITS!

Time is on your side at your age. So while you might be wishing you could snap your fingers to suddenly turn 25, adults want to snap their fingers to go back in time.

To understand why I say this, you should know about Compound Interest and the Time Value of Money.

Maybe you've heard the term 'compound interest' before but didn't realize what it was.

Say you put $1000.00 into an investment account with 10% annual interest. That means you'll make 10% of the $1,000.00 you put into the account after a year passes.

Year One: $1000 x 0.10 = $100

You've made $100 after one year. You can get a dividend payment of that amount and wait to cash in for another $100 the following year, OR, you can rely on compounding interest to make you some extra cash.

Let's say you keep the $1,100 in savings for another year and keep the original investment plus the dividends in savings for 5 years.

Year Two: $1,100 x 0.10 = $110
Year Three: $1,210 x 0.10 = $121
Year Four: $1,331 x 0.10 = $133.1
Year Five: $1,464.1 x 0.10 = $146.41

Time to compare. If you took the dividend of $100 out every year for five years, you would have earned a total of $500 in interest. But if you let the money compound in interest, you will total $610.51.

The more money you put in, the more you make back in interest.

The Time Value of Money is a concept that incorporates three separate components:

Risk, Inflation, and Liquidity.

This concept states that money is worth more today than it is in the future, and it's always based on its earning potential. As time continues its steady, marching pace into the future, more money will be needed to survive than you need now. It's how our world works, which is why I want you to set your finances up well in advance. What you pay $10 for today might cost $50 in 5 years. (shrugs) When you figure out how to snap your fingers and make it rain gold, let me know, would ya?

GENERAL TIPS ON SAVING.

- Cut back on ordering take out and deliveries.
- Avoid using credit. You'll want a low debt-to-credit ratio. When you're old enough to get your first credit card, keep the charges low and don't buy anything you can't completely pay off that month. This will boost that credit for you.

- Regularly save no matter what.
- Don't spend impulsively. Make yourself conscious of every purchase, so you don't overindulge and develop bad habits leading to missing rent payments.
- When you're in a bad mood and want to indulge, do so at home with a pint of Ben and Jerry's, not by blowing your entire budget for the month at the mall.
- If you are buying stuff just to fit in with certain friends, you need to be mature enough to evaluate if these are really your people. Remember to be authentic. Your wallet will thank you.
- Find discounts and use them!
- Build credit by remaining employed consistently, get a secured credit card, and keep big loans down to avoid impacting your life.
- Protect your assets by reading all documents and statements, keeping your personal information hidden, and always setting up password protection.

Getting a job, learning to make a budget, saving, and investing is A LOT to take in. Please don't feel rushed or pressured to feel like you need to have it all figured out right away. This is a section of life learning that requires diligence and time. So, do your research, talk to your parents, speak with financial advisors, and enjoy those Starbucks lattes you've reasoned into your budget!

Up next, we move from the world of money and into your home world: *Managing a House on Your Own.*

MANAGING THE HOUSE ON YOUR OWN

"Having a simplified, uncluttered home is a form of self-care."

— EMMA SCHEIB

L iving on your own will be the most exciting, rewarding, and maybe even scariest part of your life. Yes, we all work to make money, but what are we working for at the end of the day? Our homes. We want to work to live, not live to work. And venturing out on your own is a huge step into the unknown of endless possibilities. So, naturally, it's going to be daunting to make the big move into your own place, but it's oh so very worth it.

Most teens first move away from home when they go to college. A lot of teenagers opt to live in dorm rooms, sorority/fraternity houses, or on-campus apartments, so they have a community of peers surrounding them. Whether or not your first experience living on your own is for education or just because it was time to leave the nest, you're going to be responsible for yourself in a way you've never been before. I want to teach you about the necessities of thriving, not just surviving, on your own. Let's go.

COOKING AND PREPARING YOUR OWN FOOD!

A lot of what we learn in the kitchen as children come in the form of, "Don't touch that!" That's hot put it down." "Don't spill it!" et cetera. And now, as a teenager, I'm sure you understand some of the reasons behind the parental paranoia of kids "helping" make meals. But now that you're mature and responsible enough to handle the dangers of a kitchen and the safe food preparation that comes with it, we need to tackle some of the basics.

All food, whether plant or animal based, is covered in bacteria and microbes. The *World Health Organization*

(WHO) has compiled a list of food safety rules to help us avoid illnesses and injuries from the food we make and eat.

1. Choose foods processed for safety. – In the US, we are lucky the FDA regulates our food. However, some other countries don't have this regulation; thus, they have higher rates of food-borne illnesses and deaths. Therefore, if given the option in a store, you should buy items sealed properly within expiration dates and pasteurized.

2. Cook food thoroughly! – Raw meats, eggs, and unpasteurized dairy are especially susceptible to pathogenic (illness-causing) strains of bacteria. Cooking your food to at least 158 degrees Fahrenheit kills these strains. Thaw meats before cooking!

3. Eat cooked food right away. – Microbes go crazy proliferating at room temperature. So once that delicious hot plate of food is served, go ahead and scarf it down.

4. Store your cooked food the right way. – Food needs to be kept hot, at least around 140 degrees Fahrenheit, or cold, around 50 degrees Fahrenheit. You want to get them to these temperatures as quickly as possible.

5. Reheat your cooked foods thoroughly. – Food will inevitably have some microbes grow during storage because proper storage only slows them down; it doesn't kill them. So when you reheat your food, make sure it reaches 158 degrees again to kill off those little germs.

6. Don't contaminate cooked food with raw food! – For example, if you use the same plate to serve the cooked turkey you had it sitting on when it was raw, that's contaminated the food. Even though we can't see bacteria, they're everywhere. The slightest contact can re-introduce disease-causing bacteria.

7. Wash your hands! – Did you touch that chicken? Wash them. Did you chop up an onion? Wash them. Did you pour a glass of milk? Wash them. Did I get my point across? Everything we touch contaminates our hands, so everything our hands touch next gets those same ubiquitous microbes. Yuck.

8. Clean all kitchen surfaces. – Even if the food didn't touch anything, particles from our food hang in the air floating back down to settle on whatever surface is closest.

9. Protect your food from animals, rodents, and insects. – I know it seems obvious, but it's one of those things we don't think about until we're

on our own. If you weren't responsible for pest control or shooing the cat off the counter, this is new for you. But animals carry disease-causing bacteria, so protect your food using proper storage techniques and containers.

BUYING AND STORING FOOD! -THIS IS THE FUN PART.

I remember grocery shopping for the first time when I lived alone. To buy my food felt so liberating. I realized I was not just growing up, but I had already made it! I want you to have the same fulfilling experience, too.

- When you get your cart at the grocery store, buy all non-frozen/refrigerated items first! You want the cold stuff to stay cold!
- Use the plastic bags provided for you to wrap meat and poultry in before placing them in the cart. Keep all meat separate from other foods you'd eat raw.
- If you have a long drive home, store the cold items in an insulated cooler.
- Before you buy eggs, check for cracks. Keep eggs refrigerated in their carton on a shelf, not in the door.

- Freeze meats you aren't going to eat for several days.
- Once opened, deli meats have a refrigerator shelf life of 3-5 days—one week for hotdogs.
- Avoid bruised fruit or fruit with broken skin.
- Any meat that's pre-stuffed, like turkey or roulades.

When buying produce, cut away bruised/browned areas before eating or cooking. Make sure you use fresh running water to clean fruits and veggies and scrub firm produce like carrots with a produce brush. Those tiny crevasses are easy hiding places for not-so-nice germs.

BUSTING SOME COOKING MYTHS.

Don't get me wrong; I'm grateful for my grandma's, grandma's, aunty's grandma's passed down and "sworn by" traditional methods of family cooking. But I'm even more grateful that scientists and researchers have perfected our methods for the sake of our health.

1. Don't wash raw meat in the sink. Microscopic water droplets flinging invisible salmonella-chicken-goo throughout your beautifully

scrubbed kitchen is not what we're going for. Ha! OK, but for real. Cook it, don't wash it.

2. Thaw or marinate meat in the refrigerator or microwave, NOT at room temperature. Remember what I mentioned about bacteria having little parties in your food at room temp?

3. Cook all meat until the juices run clear when pressed.

4. Egg white should be firm and white when cooked properly. None of that booger-y stuff should be left behind. Even scrambled eggs need to be cooked through and not runny. To cover all bases, no foods with any amount of raw egg are safe to eat. Yes, sadly, this includes cookie dough, and I can't even begin to tell you how upset that makes me.

USING A MEAT THERMOMETER.

If you want to save time and avoid emergency room trips, may I suggest (drum roll) the Meat Thermometer! You must cook food to its proper temperature to keep yourself and your family from getting sick. When you use a thermometer, the tip will go into the thickest part but away from bones or fat. Of course, make sure you wash it between uses.

- Red meat and pork (whole cuts). Cook to 145°F and rest for 3 minutes before carving or eating.
- Poultry. Cook to 165ºF.
- Ground red meat and pork. Cook to 160ºF.
- Egg-based dishes. Cook to 160ºF.
- ALL leftovers. Cook to a minimum of 165ºF.

POST-MEAL KNOWLEDGE: CLEANING.

I think I already hammered home the need to wash your hands and everything food touches. But I have a few more tidbits of cleaning advice.

1. Leftovers shouldn't be eaten after more than four days.
2. Clean surfaces and all dishware with warm soapy water or in the dishwasher.
3. Discard tattered cutting boards. Those old knife grooves harbor a ton of bacteria that's difficult to wash away.
4. Pitch old sponges. Buy a bulk pack to easily switch them out weekly.

EXPIRATION DATES.

Checking expiration dates is a habit you'll want to form while buying your groceries and before using anything you have at home. In the US, we don't have a totally standardized system for dating foods, so there are a few ways to interpret the "good-by" dates on packaging.

- Sell By: The date on the package is roughly 1/3 of the item's shelf life once you take it home.
- Use By: This is a suggested date for when the food should be eaten. It doesn't necessarily mean eating the food slightly after that date will cause illness, but it will be up to your discernment to use the product past that point.
- Best If Used By/Before: These dates are used for quality assurance, meaning the food item is tastiest with the highest quality. Anytime past the date, good quality is not guaranteed.
- Freeze By: This date is used to maintain the food's quality at its peak. This is not a safety warning/date.

WRAPPING IT UP WITH KITCHEN SAFETY.

If I counted the number of times I thought I absolutely knew what I was doing, but karma decided to show me otherwise -long whistle- that list would be a mile long.

1. Keep an eye on what you're cooking. We live in a world that makes it easy to get distracted, but

serious problems can arise from kitchen accidents. Don't let that water boil over, or the oven pre-heat with an old pizza box still in there.

2. Try to use the backburners and turn the handles inward. Running into a pot handle poking over the edge of the stove and sending a cascade of scalding spaghetti sauce down your front is the last thing you were probably looking forward to. But, again, we're creating those good habits.

3. Knives are a kitchen essential, so using them safely is a must!! Try using the "bear claw" method when holding the item you're carving. Keep your fingertips pointing down and curled to avoid cutting yourself. When you're peeling or cutting, do so by pointing the blade and moving it away from your body.

4. Don't put aluminium foil, or anything metal, into a microwave. But if you're curious about what'll happen, look it up on YouTube.

5. Like metals, Don't EVER, under any circumstances, heat plain water in the microwave. Microwaves work by interacting with water molecules in such a way that they heat very rapidly. When the cup is moved, it can

explode, sending boiling water everywhere. You've been warned, my friend.

Since we're on the topic of safety and potential dangers....

How to Handle a Kitchen Fire.

If this ever happens, I want you to find that strong inner self and go through these steps one by one. Practice really does make perfect, and your safety is not something to gamble with, so take some time to work through this scenario.

- If an adult is present, call out to one immediately.
- Use baking soda to smother small flames. If flames are inside a pan on the stove, cover it with a lid to cut off its oxygen supply.
- If the flames are too large, leave the house immediately and dial 911.
- Fire Extinguishers can be used if you know what you're doing. The Fire Chief at your local station can check yours annually or semi-annually to ensure it's in good condition.

144 | ROBERT JAMES RYAN

- Use the acronym PASS to remember the steps.

1. PULL the pin out.
2. AIM at the base of the flames.
3. SQUEEZE the handle.
4. SWEEP using the nozzle aimed at the base of the flames back and forth.

*Disclaimer- Do not use a fire extinguisher without being trained. Ask your parents to go over this with you. *

Basic First Aid.

In life, we can expect bumps and bruises along the way! So if -or really when- you find yourself in need of basic medical attention for minor cuts/ scrapes, burns, eye injuries, or from ingesting something toxic, this is a good starting place.

1. Small cuts and scrapes should be cleaned with warm soap and water. Depending on the cut, you might apply pressure to stop the bleeding. Add a small dab of antibacterial ointment to the area and cover it with a bandage or gauze with tape.

*Go to the emergency room if bleeding is severe or doesn't stop after 5-10 minutes of pressure. *

You may need to visit a doctor if the cut becomes infected or is longer than ½ inch.

2. There are different types -known as degrees- of burns. They range in severity, with first-degree burns being the least severe, to third-degree burns, which is a medical emergency. For treating minor burns at home, immediately run the area under cold water for 3-5 minutes to decrease the swelling. Take off any clothing surrounding the burn unless the cloth is stuck to the burn.

Only use antibiotic ointment and a clean bandage to cover the burn. I don't mean to disappoint my grandma's grandma's aunt's grandma, who passed down their "secret recipe" of rubbing butter or oil on a burn, but that inflames and infects the wound further. Sorry, Nana.

*Use discernment when treating second-degree burns; you may need to visit a doctor. You must go to the emergency room for third-degree burns as soon as possible. *

3. If you accidentally get vinegar or a toxic cleaning reagent splashed into your eye(s), keep calm, and make your way to the sink.

- Allow a gentle stream of lukewarm water to rinse over your eye(s).

- Continue this for 15 minutes. I know it seems excessive, but it's necessary.
- If irritation continues, call your doctor.
- Check with the National Poison Control Center at 1-800-222-1222.

If you've cut your eye, don't wash it or apply pressure!!! Call 911.

If something is stuck in your eyes, don't touch or rub it!!! Call 911.

4. If you know -or even think- you swallowed something poisonous, call the National Poison Control Center at 1-800-222-1222, THEN call 911. I want you to contact the NPCC because they will know exactly what you should do for the specific substance you took. This is their specialty, and they're available to help you in these situations. Finally, you must go to the hospital, even if you aren't entirely sure if you ingested something poisonous. Once again, your life is not something to be gambled!!

*Take the chemical or product to the hospital so the emergency room staff will know how to treat you best. *

IN CASE OF EMERGENCY.

When you first move out, the medical supplies your family used to keep you safe will probably stay with them -I'm assuming. A first aid kit is one of the crucial things you'll want to buy and keep updated and stocked throughout the year. You can always add items you think are necessary, giving you a good starting place.

- A current First-Aid manual. READ it! Please don't buy it and let it sit there until there's an emergency!
- Make a list of emergency phone numbers. You can also log this information into your cell phone.
- Sterile gauze pads, Band-Aids, and adhesive tape - all in multiple sizes.
- Elastic bandages and a splint.
- Antiseptic wipes, alcohol wipes, soap, hand sanitizer, rubbing alcohol, and hydrogen peroxide.

Hydrogen peroxide should be used sparingly. It can kill healthy tissue with continued exposure

- Sterile water, saline solution, and a large syringe for washing cuts.

- Tweezers, sharp scissors, and safety pins.
- Instant cold and heat packs.
- A thermometer.
- Tooth preservation kit * *If you knock out a tooth, do NOT touch the roots of the tooth with your fingers. You can put the tooth in a glass of milk if you don't have a kit and immediately see a dentist.* *
- Non-latex gloves (several pairs)
- A flashlight with extra batteries, a radio, and a phone charger.
- A CPR mouthpiece. *Do not administer breath CPR without oral protection. It is not worth risking your life by putting your mouth to that of a stranger. Recent upgrades in medicine teach to use hand-over-hand chest compressions to the beat of "Stayin' Alive" by the Bee Gees instead of rescue breaths.* *
- Eye wash solution.

OVER THE COUNTER (OTC) MEDICATIONS TO KEEP ON HAND.

- Antibiotic ointments, such as Neosporin or Bacitracin.
- Hydrocortisone cream (1%), and calamine lotion.
- Acetaminophen and Ibuprofen.

- Benadryl, Zyrtec, or any store brand names for antihistamines.
- Cough drops and cold medications like Day/Nyquil
- Bismuth tablets (Pepto-Bismol)
- Loperamide
- Medicine syringes and cups.
- Always order extra prescription medications when traveling.

REAL-LIFE MEDICAL EMERGENCIES AND HOW TO HANDLE THEM.

DISCLAIMER! Before I begin this section, I want to clarify that I am not a medical professional. You should always consult a physician or dial 911 for any medical emergency. This is also the case if you feel any situation is beyond your capability to handle safely. If you are ever questioning a situation, always err on the side of caution and call 911 for assistance.

Any of the information I am providing in this section should only be used once you have been instructed by an appropriate and licensed medical professional and certified in a Basic Life Support (BLS) class. This section should only be used as an informative guide to help you brush up on your training.

ADMINISTERING CARDIOPULMONARY RESUSCITATION (CPR).

CPR is a technique used to save someone's life who has suffered an event such as a heart attack or might have almost drowned, where their breathing and heartbeat have stopped. As you can imagine, this enormous responsibility often induces stress in the rescuer. Once you've completed your BLS class, this is a good refresher to follow.

1. Gentle shake the victim and loudly ask, "Are you OK?"
2. Call 911 IMMEDIATELY or ask someone nearby to call. Do this BEFORE you begin CPR.
3. If you do not have a CPR breath protector, you will only do chest compressions. Here's why: Lungs hold residual oxygen, but without the heart to pump it through the body, it does the victim no good. So your best bet is to stick to chest compressions. *Your compressions force the blood through the heart manually when it cannot beat on its own.*
4. Overlap your hands, the heel of your dominant hand pressing down into the middle of the sternum. Straighten your arms and position your body above your hands over the victim's

sternum. Your knees should be bent and on the ground.

5. You'll use the force and weight of your body to apply pressure 2 inches down into the sternum and rise back up again at a rate of 100 compressions per minute. Sing the Bee Gees song "Stayin' Alive" to keep up a good rhythm.

6. Make sure to position their chin tilted backward so that the victim's airway is open. If you have a CPR breath protector, pinch their nostrils closed, place the card over their mouth, tilt their chin down, and give two full rescue breaths of one second each.

7. Continue this cycle until medical help arrives.

USING THE HEIMLICH MANOEUVRE.

This lifesaving technique uses physical, forceful pressure to dislodge an item caught in a victim's throat which can no longer breathe. Unless your BLS class covers and certifies you for Heimlich techniques on pregnant women and infants, the method outlined here is only to be done on a non-pregnant person. Always dial 911 for a medical emergency.

1. Help the choking victim to stand up while you position yourself behind them.

2. Assist them in leaning forward and bracing themselves with both hands on a hard surface. Then, use the heel of your free hand to deliver five consecutive blows to their mid back just below their shoulder blades.

3. Bring both of your arms around their waist. With one hand, place a fist just above the navel with the thumb side in. Use your other hand to grab your fist. In one swift motion, thrust your fist in and upward simultaneously.

4. Perform these abdominal thrusts five times!

5. Repeat this process until the object is expelled and the person can breathe or begins to cough on their own.

The Heimlich Manoeuvre on Yourself! *(Yes, this is a real thing)*

Like the outline provided above but done -quite literally- on yourself by yourself.

1. Make a fist and place it above your navel, thumb side tucked in.

2. Grab your fist with the other hand, thrusting inward and upward simultaneously.

3. Repeat until the object you're choking on is expelled and you can breathe or cough.

*You are also using the back of a chair or a hard flat object to thrust your abdomen into instead of using your hands. *

SUPPORTING A SPRAIN AND STRAIN.

If you've ever played sports or watched them, you're probably familiar with the terms "sprain" and "strain." You might not have known what those are, but you knew they're some form of injury via context clues. And you'd be right because, yes, they are.

A *sprain* is an injury to the ligaments (the fibrous tissue connecting bones), whereas a *strain* is an injury to a muscle or tendon (the fibrous tissue connecting muscles to bone). Before I learned anatomy, I had never given these terms a second thought. Looking back, did I think bones and muscles were free-floating in the body? It's a good example of "you don't know what you don't know."

Use the R.I.C.E Method!

1. REST the injured area/limb. This is your body; it is your fortress. If it hurts, it hurts. Stop whatever you're doing and take care of it.
2. ICE the area. Do NOT use heat. Heat will cause more inflammation, thus more pain.

3. COMPRESS the injured area with an elastic wrap or bandage. DO NOT RUB OR STRETCH!! An injury to soft tissue is a series of tears, the severity ranging from microscopic to complete tears. If you rub or stretch the injury, it will make it worse. Instead, you want to stabilize this area to allow healing to occur.

4. ELEVATE the injured area above your heart to limit or prevent swelling.

HOW TO SPOT A CONCUSSION.

At your age, you're cognitively and intuitively aware of innate human behavior. You can tell if someone seems off, like if you notice someone at school has a black eye. That's not normal, and it's suspicious. If you ask them if they're OK, they might tell you they're fine and try to avoid you. Maybe they pretend everything is normal, but clearly, there's a problem. You can feel that you need to let a teacher or trusted adult know so they can get your friend the help they need to keep them safe.

The same goes for head injuries such as concussions. There will be signs that something is wrong, but they might not be able to communicate that to you. You must listen to your gut. If you're unsure what it is you should be looking and listening for, here is a list of several signs and symptoms you might observe in a person with a head concussion. If you have the faintest hint that there might be an issue, seek emergency medical assistance immediately.

Symptoms You Might Observe.

- If a person can't recall events prior to or after a hit or a fall.
- If they appear dazed or stunned.
- Forgetting instructions or seeming confused about regular assignments. If it's during a sports game and they don't understand what position they play, etc.
- Moves awkwardly or seems suddenly clumsy.
- Answers questions with slurred speech, slowly, or delayed.
- Loses consciousness (even for a split second).
- Has mood, behavior, or personality changes.
- Their taste and smell is suddenly disordered or different.

Symptoms They Might Report.

- Having a headache or pressure built up in their head.
- Their ears begin ringing.
- If they're nauseous or vomiting.

- Have balance problems or feel dizzy/blurry vision.
- Having spots or "stars" in their vision.
- Irritated by light or noises.
- Feeling sluggish, hazy, or foggy.
- Confusion or memory problems.
- Feeling "off" or "down."

There are many ways a concussion can manifest, which is why you must learn to tap into your intuition. If something seems off, call for help. As a teenager moving into adulthood, it is your responsibility to learn how to care for yourself and others. It's not a burden so much as it is a privilege.

I hope you're never in a situation that requires this level of emergency medical training, but sometimes we can't help what happens. That's why I suggest you practice, even after you take a class. These situations are rare, so it's easy for the procedure to fade out of your mind after some time has passed. Try to stay on top of it.

Pro Tip: Many teenagers get stuck trying to pick a career path. You might not know everything this big ol' world has to offer. That's why classes like BLS can get you out of your comfort zone to learn something new, but it also might introduce you to the world of modern medicine. Who knows, maybe you will discover your life path is to become a paramedic, medical laboratory scientist, nurse, or doctor!

Now is a good time to take a break from the heavy and move on to something simple, yet essential....

LEARNING YOUR LAUNDRY!

Keeping your clothes clean is one area that can easily fall through the cracks once you're living on your own. You don't realize how quickly those dirty clothes pile up when mom isn't doing your laundry anymore. That is until you're rummaging through a week-old hamper full of stinky clothes, desperately trying to find the least wrinkled, smelly item you can throw on before you leave for work.

Think about what you wear to school every day or what you'd wear to an interview. How you present yourself in different situations is important because how you look and smell greatly impacts your self-confidence. And not only does your appearance affect you, but it influences others around you also.

You might already be familiar with laundering your clothes, but knowing some extra tips and tricks can help you save time and money. The list of laundry items you'll want to keep is relatively short; each has directions printed on the package, so make sure you familiarize yourself with each one you buy.

Laundry Detergent
Fabric Softener
Bleach/Non-chlorine bleach

On-the-Fly Laundry Hacks. *(You're welcome in advance)*

- Each item of clothing purchased from stores in the US have laundry tags adorned with symbols. These symbols are instructions for caring for that item. Print out a 'Laundry Symbols' list and keep it with you while you do laundry.
- Sort your clothes by color, fabric type, and soil level.
- If you need to bleach clothing, to avoid damaging materials, fill up the washer halfway with water before you add the bleach. Don't add the clothing until the water and bleach are mixed well.
- Pre-treat stains before washing! If you don't have a pre-treater handy, use baby wipes for the time being. Soak the item in COLD water for ~20 minutes and wash it with the rest of the load.

Use rubbing alcohol or hairspray to remove ink, then rinse with cold water.

Hydrogen peroxide will bubble blood right out of clothing.

Dish detergent and stain remover take out food grease.

Rinse chocolate or tomato-based foods with cold water and then treat with a stain remover.

- Wash clothes inside out and take everything out of the pockets! 1. This protects clothing from getting stained from anything left in its pockets. 2. The dirtiest part of the clothing is what's touching our skin, so it washes best when turned inside out.
- Close zippers to avoid catching and ripping more delicate fabrics in the wash. Anything with Velcro should also be closed.
- Don't let laundry sit in the washer. Instead, move it to the dryer or a clothesline to prevent mildew and foul odors.
- The faster you take the laundry out of the dryer, the fewer wrinkles you fight with later.
- If you shrink a sweater in the washer (especially wool, cashmere, or mohair), do NOT transfer it to a dryer. It'll seal its shrunken fate. Instead, grab a large tub, heavy bath towels, stainless-

steel T-shaped pins, cool water, baby shampoo or liquid fabric softener, and a cork bulletin board.

Fill the tub with water, add two tablespoons of baby shampoo or fabric softener, and mix.
Add the sweat and soak for 30 minutes. Remove it, and do not rinse!! Instead, gently squeeze out the mixture and roll the sweater in a towel to soak up excess water.
Pin the sweater back into its original shape on the corkboard! Let it dry in the dark, and repeat the process as needed. Voila!

SEWING A BUTTON.

It might not sound like something you'll ever worry about, but it's come in handy more times than I care to admit. Throwing away a nice shirt because a button or two popped off is ridiculous. Grab yourself a pack of buttons, some needles, and thread, and let's go!

1. Carefully thread your needle, pulling 3-4 inches of threat through the eye, and let it hang. Then, tie a sturdy knot at the very end of your string.
2. Center the button over the right area and poke the needle from the inside of the shirt (or

whatever clothing item you're sewing) up through one of the buttonholes until the knot at the end of the string engages with the fabric.

3. Threat the needle through the hole on the opposite side and down through the fabric, repeating this process for the third and fourth holes. You'll notice you're forming an 'X' with the thread.

4. When finished, flip the shirt over, thread the needle through it without going through the button, and wrap the thread around the base of the button.

5. Finish with a knot at the back.

After covering many stressful -yet rewarding- medical topics and household essentials, I think you've earned a *brake* (pun intended) before we *roll* (Yes, another pun. You're welcome) into our next topic of *Being Car Care Aware.*

BEING CAR CARE AWARE

"Your body is like a car. It will get you to your destination, but it requires care and maintenance to run well."

— UNKNOWN.

The first time you sit in the driver's seat, your palms sweat. The buzz of nervous excitement extends to each finger and toe as you grasp the wheel and take in the driver's side perspective. You've been in a car more times than you can count, but this is new. Everything feels different; it doesn't seem familiar anymore. Realizing the weight of your newfound freedom substantially boosts your confidence, and it should! When you earn the right to drive a car, you've developed a new level of maturity and responsibility.

Driving gives you independence and freedom, and honestly, it helps your parents tremendously. Once you have your driver's license, you can drive to school, extracurricular activities, work, and to your friends' houses. It opens your schedule because before you can drive, you rely on other people to get you to and from these activities, which means working around their schedules.

While you go through your learning permit phase before driving solo with a state driver's license, let me say something for you to always carry with you while you're on the road:

DRIVE RESPONSIBLY!

Cars and motor vehicles are weapons. They are the leading cause of death in the teenage population every year. Motor vehicles kill more people per year than guns.

If you want to grow up, you can't stick your head in the sand and pretend those real-world statistics don't exist. So I want you to carefully go through this list, so you can completely understand the risks you're taking with your own life and the lives of others every single time you turn on that engine. Statistics take a while to calculate, so some of these values will be from previous years.

SCARY STATISTICS. YEP, YOU NEED TO KNOW THIS.

1. Every day, 8-11 teenagers die from motor vehicle crashes. The leading cause of these deaths is TEXTING and DRIVING. If these teens knew that they would kill someone or themselves that day from texting, they never would have done it in the first place. Please understand this because it does happen, and it can happen to anyone. Yes, including you. So please, PLEASE, put your phone down. There is no text message on the face of this planet more precious than life.

2. In 2020, more than 227,000 teenagers were injured in motor vehicle collisions. Death is horrible, but so is becoming paralyzed, losing a limb(s), losing your eyes, or being burned.

3. The age range of 13-19 cost $40.7 billion* in medical costs and cost estimates for lives lost in 2020 from motor vehicle crashes. These

injuries are not little scrapes and bruises we're talking about here.

4. The age range between 16-19 years old is most responsible for crashes than any other age group. The fatal crash rate is 3 times higher per mile driven than drivers 20 years or older.

5. Passenger deaths in 2018 reached a whopping 63% due to drivers ages 16-19.

There isn't a lot of finessing I can do to make these statistics sound better. They're scary for a reason. Every driver on the road has their own life, and their lives matter to them just as much as your life matters to you. So, if you're wondering why we'd allow teenagers to drive knowing these statistics are accurate, it's because of *time*. Time is moving forward at its slow pace, and before you know it, you're going to be 18 years old. It would be best if you started learning to drive and take care of yourself now so that by the time you reach adulthood, you're ready to hit the ground running. We want you to be prepared and understand what to expect when you're out there.

RISK FACTORS.

OK, so let's talk about *why* these statistics exist. What are the risk factors that make teenage drivers so dangerous? Let's take a look.

- Inexperience. It's not your fault that you don't know everything, and no one expects you to. But I remember a saying: "If you pick up a knife by the blade, it becomes a weapon from which you'll cut yourself. On the other hand, if you pick it up by the handle, you now have a tool you can use to make life easier. The choice is yours." This information is the handle of the knife I'm trying to hand you. You can use it to make yourself safer without experiencing the pain and suffering others before you have gone through to find out the hard way.
- Nighttime and weekend driving. It's obviously harder to see at night, but nocturnal animals also venture onto the roads during this time. Teenagers ages 16-19 have 3 times more crashes at night than adults 30-59. While teenagers are off school during the weekend, it's no surprise that most accidents caused by teenagers occur between Friday and Sunday.

- Not wearing a seatbelt. I really can't wrap my mind around this one. Get in the habit of putting it on the second you sit down. There isn't one good reason, not one, as to why this shouldn't be the first thing you do, even before you start your car. It doesn't make you cool to have it off, so put it on. As a person who's been in serious car collisions, I'm alive because I was wearing a seatbelt. Put. It. On. *Lovingly shakes you by the shoulders*

- Distracted driving. Once again, it can never be said too much; texting in the car is a no-no. Texting increases your risk of crashing by 23 times. Don't gamble on those odds because one day, those odds may not be in your favor. *Whistles the hunger game mocking jay cry* Other forms of distracted driving are looking at something outside and inside of the vehicle, grooming yourself (why? Just why...), singing/dancing to music, and reaching for something you dropped.

- Speeding. I, too, love the thrill and rush of speed.... on a rollercoaster....at a theme park. I love a good adrenaline rush, but not by recklessly speeding, endangering the lives of others and myself. There's a reason speed limits exist. And yes, they're mandatory, not suggestions.

- Drinking alcohol/using drugs. I'm rolling my eyes here because we know teenagers might sneak and drink alcohol or try drugs. We're not dumb. Many adults now look back at times they tried drinking and driving when they were teenagers, too. Some of them went to jail, lost their licenses, or died. So, I'm asking you to be honest. I want you to step into your integrity and make a vow to yourself right now. If you ever know you can't drive home because you're intoxicated, but you're afraid of missing curfew and getting in trouble. Know that I speak for all parents when I say this: The pride and admiration we will have for you if you call and ask us for help if you're in this situation is enough to get you out of trouble. We're going to feel relief. It shows us that we can trust you to make good decisions, even in a tough situation. We're going to know we can have open and honest conversations. Some teenagers will want to try things, but it's worse when it's done in the dark behind our backs. Just be honest. We want you alive. I don't think this is asking too much, do you?

STAYING "SAFE" ON THE ROAD.

I put "safe" in quotations because whenever I hear someone say, "keep our roads safe," it implies that the roads are already safe, so keep them that way. Just to be clear, the roads are NOT safe. Understanding that right off the bat will help you learn the rules of the road faster. What we mean by "safe" is keeping the risk of motor vehicle collisions as low as possible. And this is true because if everyone used their best judgment and followed the best driving practices, we would significantly lower the risks on the road. Take some time to read through these ways to reduce driving risks and improve the roads.

1. Your first car as a teenager might be (not always) a hand-me-down clunker from a family member or a used car. This is because, as we mentioned before, teens are more likely to wreck, and you haven't worked to earn yourself a nice brand-new car yet. When you do choose your first car, no matter when that is in your life, consider staying away from high horsepower engines that tempt even the best drivers to push the speed limits.
2. Bigger, heavier vehicles are better protected in a crash. So check safety rating on vehicles

before making a purchase.

3. Buy a car with electronic stability control (ESC). This built-in feature will help you maintain control of your vehicle on slippery, curvy, icy, roads to reduce risks. The value of a car with ESC is compared to the value of seatbelts!

4. Respect traffic rules. Police patrol for a reason. They know humans can be selfish and thoughtless at times, so this is a great time to practice mindfulness and consideration.

5. Respect pedestrians. There's no getting around this. Pedestrians have the right of way all the time.

6. Keep an eye on your blind spots. Never merge or turn without looking.

7. Check your car's condition regularly. Maintenance isn't an option. If you want your car to work for you, you must protect and take care of it.

8. Plan ahead! Know how long it takes to get to your destination and leave early to avoid unexpected delays. Rushing, swerving, and speeding through traffic isn't fair to other drivers. It's YOUR responsibility to stick to the schedule, and no one's life is yours to gamble

with selfishly. If you're late, you're late. You still drive the speed limit and follow traffic laws.

9. Use. Your. Turn. Signals. Just like wearing your seatbelt -and Nike- Just DO IT!

10. If you're upset, tired, angry, or frustrated, the road is not the place to release those feelings. There are many options to get angst off your chest, but wrapping your car around a telephone pole or plowing into the back of someone's van full of children is not it, fam.

11. For the love of everything Holy, do not pick up hitchhikers or anyone asking for a ride who you don't know. I can't get into every scenario that could transpire in this situation, but they're not good. If you're comfortable and your parents allow, please research the law and homicide cases surrounding hitchhikers. *Shudders from the heebee jeebees. *

CAR MAINTENANCE 101.

Whether your car is brand-spankin' new or an old clunker, you should be grateful for the opportunity you've been given. Either way, you'll learn why and how maintenance is vital to prevent potentially dangerous issues from arising by keeping your car running well.

1. Flat tires happen and can happen often. First, make sure your car has a spare tire or at the very least, a "donut." Grab yourself a tool kit and a good and functional jack rated for your specific vehicle. Either a parent, autobody store employee, repair facility or dealership can help show you how to change a flat properly. If you find yourself with a flat tire without a spare or tools for the job, dialing your insurance company or AAA will help you with roadside assistance.

2. Over and underinflated tires are dangerous, not just something to ignore. If the tire bursts while you're driving, it can become easy to lose control of the vehicle and potentially crash. Ask a parent or vehicle professional to teach you how to use a tire pressure check to ensure the tires are properly inflated. The PSI levels for your car should be found by opening the driver's side door and checking the tag at the bottom. If tires look worn or bald, change them as soon as possible.

3. There are several fluids your car uses to run efficiently, so checking to make sure their levels are sufficient is a must. Oil, windshield wiper fluid, antifreeze, and power steering fluid levels should only be checked when the car is turned

off and parked on a flat, level surface. The car's owner manual will have the proper procedures for checking and changing these fluids.

4. Jump-starting a car is knowledge every driver on the road needs. Both vehicles should be in park or neutral, and the hoods should be close to one another. Make sure they're turned off and both have their parking brakes engaged.

- Clamp the RED (positive) cable onto the disabled vehicle's red (positive) battery terminal FIRST.

- At the other end of the cables is another red cable that you will clamp to the car's red battery terminal, which will do the jump-start.

- Now clamp the BLACK (negative) cable to the black battery terminal on the car, providing the jump-start.

- Finally, the black clamp can be clamped to any large, metal surface without any paint anywhere in the engine bay, but away from the battery and engine itself. After the cables are connected, turn on the vehicle providing the jump-start, then begin trying to start the vehicle needing the jump. Once it starts, allow both to run for 3 minutes. You'll want to keep that car turned on until you can make it to an auto repair store.

STEPS TO TAKE WHEN PULLED OVER BY THE POLICE.

It's easy for me to say, "don't be nervous," while I'm writing this, comfortably lounging in my favorite chair casually sipping coffee. But, of course, you'll be nervous in that situation. Even I still get nervous jitters when I see those flashing lights. So take a deep breath, remind yourself it isn't the end of the world, and take these tips step by step. You're going to be OK.

1. Once you see those lights behind you and the realization you're being pulled over hits you, don't panic. Instead, let yourself remember that this is a normal situation that happens. But first, turn on your hazard lights.

2. Pull over to a safe spot. In driving school, the method taught to us is to make your way onto the right-hand shoulder. However, since the police officer must get out of his car next to a road, it might be nicer if you slowly pull off the road into a gas station or fast-food parking area if possible. I even pulled off to the left shoulder into a grassy median, and the officer thanked

me for the consideration. I got off with a warning to fix my taillight instead of a ticket.

3. Be very cautious if you're getting pulled over by an unmarked vehicle. Some predators sometimes impersonate police officers with the intent of robbing (or worse) the unsuspecting victim. If the car doesn't look like something an officer of the law would be driving, you can dial 911, explain the situation, and ask them to send another officer to your location. If it really is a police officer pulling you over, they'll understand the situation and validate your concern. If it's a predator, they'll not want the police involved, and their behavior will reflect this.

4. Roll down your window, have your license and insurance card in hand, but keep your hands on the steering wheel where the officer can see them. If it's nighttime, turn on the overhead dome light, so you're visible.

5. If you reach for anything, you need to inform the officer before you do so and let them know what it is you're reaching for. I have a buddy who reached toward his glovebox for his registration records during a routine stop without informing the officer. As a result, he wound up handcuffed up against his car. People

wound and kill police officers for doing their jobs, so don't give them a reason to suspect you of anything of ill-intent.

6. Stay calm and follow the officer's instructions—point blank, period. Be polite, and say "yes ma'am or no sir" when responding to their questions as signs of respect.

7. Read your constitutional rights. I mean it. You have a right to know what police officers are and are not allowed to do within their scope of practice.

8. Come to an agreement. If the officer catches you speeding and they prove this on their radar, you're allowed to ask for a pass, especially if it's your first time. Let them know you won't speed again or roll a stop sign and that this has been a learning experience. However, if you do it again, you're getting a ticket. Sorry about it. Don't say I didn't warn you.

9. If given a ticket, sign it. But don't be a brat and argue. Officers can make notes of your driving history so other officers can read it in the future if they pull you over.

10. You're always allowed to ask for other officers or supervisors to be present. The more witnesses are present, the better. You never know what can save your skin or theirs.

Driving is a privilege earned through responsibility, respect for yourself and other drivers, and proper vehicle maintenance. So take it nice and slow. Practice makes perfect. Be patient with other drivers, obey traffic laws, and be polite and cooperative with police officers. Enjoy this new freedom. You've earned it!

CONCLUSION

There are so many adventures in this beautiful life you're creating. Now that you've begun your journey into your teenage years take the knowledge you've learned so far and apply it with ease and grace. It's a lot, I know, but you have the tools you need to propel yourself farther than you can imagine.

You're discovering what it takes to get to know yourself. You're building a sturdy foundation of self-trust and belief. Following your intuition only leads to discovering your passions while learning to stand up for what you believe is best for you. This inner love, when tended to, bolsters the ability to live a healthy lifestyle, manage your time, and sort your priorities. Even with these skills, are challenges still going to arise? You bet. But you better believe that when you balance your life, you'll be able to handle these issues like a bull charging a flag.

Remember, you're not alone in this teenage transition. Every other teen on this big ol' planet is feeling this shift, these changes that make you feel like an island. But you're not alone! Learning to strengthen your social skills and building bonds fortifies not only yourself but the relationships that will carry you farther into your future. And in the relationships you're building, you'll know how to have each other's backs when you smell trouble. Then, when you find yourself, you'll find your people.

You're aware now of how to be cautious online with potential scams, predators, and hackers. Part of the responsibility of growing up is admitting when you don't know something or need help. If you feel uncomfortable, protect yourself and find an adult to help. You're an intelligent, wonderful person who values yourself. Don't ever let someone pressure you into something. Remember, take that deep breath, and stand your ground. You've got this.

Landing your first job is an enormous victory and a reason to celebrate! It's OK if you're still making a plan before you put it into action. It's the effort and responsibility you're taking that count! I'm so proud of you for getting this far. Enjoy the accomplishments and treat yo'self, just not too much. *wink* Save some of that money in one of the investment accounts we talked about. Develop strategies to grow your money now, so you're ready for the future. Oh, how you'll thank me later.

Once you've taken that leap of faith into the new and you're managing the house on your own, try not to forget to eat some vegetables occasionally, would ya? Read through the section for proper food temperatures as many times as you need. And you might not memorize the list of every laundry tag meaning, so go ahead and print one out to save yourself time...and shrunken cashmere sweaters.

If you ever face an emergency medical situation and don't have the steps or skills to handle a situation, ALWAYS dial 911 for emergency assistance. Keep calm and do your best with the information you have, but let medical professionals assist when and where appropriate. But for your list of household medical supplies, use the list I provided, get into a BLS course, and brush up on your knowledge, so you don't get rusty. If you don't use it, it'll be easy to lose it.

Keep up with those car care and driving basics! Your parents wish they could bubble wrap you, but that isn't feasible, so we'll settle for careful, considerate driving and always wearing a seat belt. Stay. Off. Of. Your. Cell.

Phone. There are dramatic hand claps between those words because I'm serious. Now that you know those statistics on vehicle collisions in your age bracket, you don't get to plead ignorant anymore. Protect yourself and others. Pretty please.

These teenage years can be challenging for you. So, I feel honored to have had the privilege to help guide you on this tremendous excursion called life, and with the help of this book, you'll prepare yourself for what lies ahead. Be patient with yourself and others. Growing up is a process; you're developing a strong backbone to face it all. I wish you a long, beautiful, happy, and healthy life. Cheers!

WAIT! BEFORE YOU GO...

If you read this book and found you learned a thing or two, you can help boost this book into the life of another teenager by giving it an honest review on Amazon. I'd appreciate it more than you know. Thank you, thank you!

NOTES

INTRODUCTION

1. "Kim Harrison Quote." *A*, https://www.azquotes.com/quote/
435324

CHAPTER 1

1. *Forbes*, Forbes Magazine, https://www.forbes.com/quotes/
2785/
2. Eva, Amy L. "Five Ways to Help Teens Build a Sense of Self-Worth." *Mindful*, 10 Jan. 2022, https://www.mindful.org/
five-ways-to-help-teens-build-a-sense-of-self-worth/
3. "Psychotherapy in Gaithersburg MD." *Washington Psychological Wellness*, 5 Oct. 2022, https://washington-psychwellness.com/
4. Staff, Beta Bowl. "Activities to Help Your Teen Discover Their Passion & Purpose: Beta Bowl." *Beta Bowl - Turning Kids into Entrepreneurs*, 1 Apr. 2021, https://beta-bowl.com/
activities-to-help-your-teen-discover-their-passion-purpose
5. *10 Ways to Find Your Passion (plus Benefits) | Indeed.com.* https://
www.indeed.com/career-advice/career-development/how-to-find-your-passion

6. "How to Handle Peer Pressure (for Kids) - Nemours Kidshealth." Edited by D'Arcy Lyness, *KidsHealth*, The Nemours Foundation, Feb. 2022, https://kidshealth.org/en/kids/peer-pressure.html

7. "How to Deal with Bullies." *NCAB*, https://www.ncab.org.au/bullying-advice/bullying-for-kids/how-to-deal-with-bullies

8. "6 Smarter Ways to Deal with a Bully." *Psychology Today*, Sussex Publishers, https://www.psychologytoday.com/us/blog/the-couch/201702/6-smarter-ways-deal-bully

CHAPTER 2

1. "Productive and Free." *Productive and Free*, https://www.productiveandfree.com/

2. *10 Ways to Find Your Passion (plus Benefits) | Indeed.com.* https://www.indeed.com/career-advice/career-development/how-to-find-your-passion

3. VanDuzer, Todd. "7 Time Management Techniques for Teens." *HuffPost*, HuffPost, 7 Dec. 2017, https://www.huffpost.com/entry/7-time-management-techniq_b_8544898

4. Morin, Amanda. "How to Help Teens Develop Good Study Habits." *Understood*, 14 Apr. 2021, https://www.understood.org/en/articles/how-to-help-your-teen-develop-good-study-habits

5. "5 Effective Study Tips for Teens & Students." *Scholars Education*, 25 Oct. 2021, https://www.scholarsed.com/study-tips-for-teens/

6. "11 Good Study Habits to Develop." *Coursera*, https://www.coursera.org/articles/study-habits

7. "How Teens Can Stay Fit." *HealthyChildren.org*, https://www.healthychildren.org/English/ages-stages/teen/fitness/Pages/How-Teens-Can-Stay-Fit.aspx

8. "Default - Stanford Medicine Children's Health." *Stanford Medicine Children's Health - Lucile Packard Children's Hospital Stanford*, https://www.stanfordchildrens.org/en/topic/default?id=exercise-and-teenagers-90-P01602

9. Kilroy, Dana Sullivan. "Fitness and Exercise: Workouts, Nutrition, and More." *Healthline*, Healthline Media, 2 Nov. 2017, https://www.healthline.com/health/fitness-exercise

10. Clifton, Tamera. "Exercise for Teenagers: How Much They Need, and How to Fit It In." *Healthline*, Healthline Media, 13 Apr. 2022, https://www.healthline.com/health/fitness/exercise-for-teenagers

11. Department of Health & Human Services. "Teenagers and Sleep." *Better Health Channel*, Department of Health & Human Services, 22 Oct. 2007, https://www.betterhealth.vic.gov.au/health/healthyliving/teenagers-and-sleep

12. Aacap. *Stress Management and Teens*, https://www.aacap.org/AACAP/Families_and_Youth/Facts_for_Families/FFF-Guide/Helping-Teenagers-With-Stress-066.aspx

13. *Resilience - American Psychological Association.* https://www. apa.org/topics/resilience/

CHAPTER 3

1. "Zig Ziglar Quotes." *BrainyQuote*, Xplore, https://www. brainyquote.com/quotes/zig_ziglar_393135

2. California, Yael KleinOriginally from. "How to Help Your Teenager Make Friends." *Evolve Treatment Centers*, 22 Sept. 2020, https://evolvetreatment.com/blog/help-teenager-make-friends/

3. Clifton, Tamera. "Exercise for Teenagers: How Much They Need, and How to Fit It In." *Healthline*, Healthline Media, 13 Apr. 2022, https://www.healthline.com/health/fitness/exercise-for-teenagers#considerations

4. Ashley Hudson LMFT. "13 Ways on How to Help Your Teen Make Friends." *Ashley Hudson LMFT*, 27 Dec. 2022, https://www.ashleyhudsontherapy.com/post/13-ways-on-how-to-help-your-teen-make-friends

5. Lisa B. Marshall of Quick and Dirty Tips. "How to Avoid Awkward Silence." *The Muse*, The Muse, 19 June 2020, https://www.themuse.com/advice/5-tips-thatll-help-you-avoid-that-dreaded-awkward-silence

6. Daniel, Pamela. "Eating out Etiquette for Teens." *Parentcircle*, Parentcircle, 18 Sept. 2020, https://localservices.parentcircle.com/article/eating-out-etiquette-for-teens/

7. Bailey, Jon. "Table Manners for Teenagers." *2 Dads with Baggage*, 23 Feb. 2021, https://2dadswithbaggage.com/table-manners-for-teenagers/

8. https://educationpossible.com/table-manners-for-teens/

9. "Antonio Centeno." *Real Men Real Style Stories*, https://www.realmenrealstyle.com/how-to-tip/

10. Jacobson, Tyler. "Stepping up Standards: 18 Manners Every Teen Needs by Age 18." *The Good Men Project*, 21 July 2022, https://goodmenproject.com/families/stepping-up-standards-18-manners-every-teen-needs-by-age-18-wcz/

11. "Teens and Romantic Relationships." *Child Mind Institute*, 2 Feb. 2023, https://childmind.org/article/how-to-help-kids-have-good-romantic-relationships/

12. Applebury, Gabrielle. "Teen Love and Dating Advice." *LoveToKnow*, LoveToKnow, 9 July 2019, https://dating.lovetoknow.com/Category:Teen_Love

13. Butler, Tamsen. "Teen Dating Advice." *LoveToKnow*, LoveToKnow, 15 July 2022, https://dating.lovetoknow.com/Teen_Dating

CHAPTER 4

1. Kanchwala, Mohammad, et al. "10 Quotes on Social Media for a Brand New Perspective: Social Samosa." *Social Samosa | Indian Social Media Knowledge Storehouse*, 29 June 2017, https://www.socialsamosa.com/2017/06/quotes-on-social-media/

2. Shteriova, Ivana. "18 Internet Safety Statistics for 2022." *Screen and Reveal*, 8 Dec. 2022, https://screenandreveal.com/ internet-safety-statistics/#:~:text=59%25%20of%20US% 20teens%20have,parents%20tracked%20their%20online% 20activity

3. "Enough Is Enough: Internet Safety." *Enough Is Enough: Internet Safety*, https://enough.org/stats_internet_safety

4. "Teens: Cyberbullying & Online Safety." *Raising Children Network*, https://raisingchildren.net.au/teens/entertainment-technology/cyberbullying-online-safety

5. "Internet Safety for Kids and Teens." *Boys & Girls Clubs of America - Providing Millions of Kids and Teens a Safe Place to Develop Essential Skills, Make Lasting Connections and Have Fun.*, https://bgca.org/news-stories/2022/December/ internet-safety-for-kids-and-teens

6. "Spending Time Online Can Be Risky!" *Kids Helpline*, 1 Dec. 2022, https://kidshelpline.com.au/teens/issues/staying-safe-online

7. "Online Safety for Teens Ages 13-18: Presentation." *Intel*, https://www.intel.com/content/www/us/en/education/ online-safety/online-safety-teens-13-18.html

8. Cyberbullying Research Center. "Sexting: Advice for Teens." *Cyberbullying Research Center*, https://cyberbullying.org/ sexting-advice-teens

CHAPTER 5

1. Quotespedia.org. "Opportunities Don't Happen. You Create Them. – Chris Grosser –..." *Quotespedia.org*, 9 Apr. 2020, https://www.quotespedia.org/authors/c/chris-grosser/opportunities-dont-happen-you-create-them-chris-grosser/

2. Stefanakos, Victoria Scanlan. "First Jobs for Teens: Help Teen Choose a Career Path and Vocation." *Understood*, 22 Oct. 2020, https://www.understood.org/en/articles/how-to-choose-the-right-job-for-your-teens-strengths

3. Grossman, Amanda L. "Teen First Job Guide: How to Prepare for Your First Job as a Teenager." *Money Prodigy*, 6 Apr. 2022, https://www.moneyprodigy.com/teen-first-job/

4. "Tips for Teenagers on Finding That First Job." *The Parents Website*, 4 Oct. 2022, https://theparentswebsite.com.au/tips-for-teenagers-on-finding-that-first-job/

5. *Indeed Career Guide | Indeed.com.* https://www.indeed.com/career-advice

6. *Resumes & Cover Letters | Indeed.com - Indeed Career Guide.* https://www.indeed.com/career-advice/resumes-cover-letters

7. Admin. "Sample Cover Letters: Cover Letter Templates: Youth Central." *Cover Letter Templates/ Youth Central*, 2 May 2017, https://www.youthcentral.vic.gov.au/jobs-and-careers/applying-for-a-job/what-is-a-cover-letter/sample-cover-letters

8. *Top 10 Tips for Teens Completing Job Applications - Las Vegas–Clark* ... https://lvccld.org/wp-content/uploads/sites/54/2021/06/TW_Basic-Info-Link-App_030819.pdf

9. Doyle, Alison. "Top Teen Job Interview Questions and Best Answers." *The Balance*, The Balance, 27 Dec. 2022, https://www.thebalancemoney.com/teen-job-interview-questions-and-best-answers-2063882

10. Frost, Alexandra. "9 Job Interview Tips for Teens." *The Muse*, The Muse, 9 Sept. 2021, https://www.themuse.com/advice/job-interview-tips-for-teens

CHAPTER 6

1. Juma, Norbert, and Master quote curator and editor on a mission to inspire. "Money Quotes Celebrating Financial Literacy and Independence." *Everyday Power*, 5 Jan. 2023, https://everydaypower.com/money-quotes/

2. "Ultimate Guide: Copper's Guide to Budgeting (for Teens)." *Ultimate Guide: Copper's Guide to Budgeting (for Teens)*, https://www.getcopper.com/guide/budgeting

3. Lake, Rebecca. "Budgeting for Teens: What You Need to Know." *The Balance*, The Balance, 5 July 2022, https://www.thebalancemoney.com/how-to-teach-your-teen-about-budgeting-4160105

4. VanSomeren, Lindsay. "How Big Should Your Emergency Fund Be?" *The Balance*, The Balance, 13 Mar. 2022, https://

www.thebalancemoney.com/is-your-emergency-fund-too-big-4142617

5. "Money Management Tips for Teens." *Credit Counselling Society*, 2 Feb. 2023, https://nomoredebts.org/budgeting/budgeting-for-teens

6. Baluch, Anna. "How to Help Your Teen Learn to Save Money." *The Balance*, The Balance, 14 July 2022, https://www.thebalancemoney.com/how-to-save-money-as-a-teenager-5204306

7. Higuera, Valencia Patrice. "How to Set up a Savings Account for a Teenager." *MyBankTracker*, MyBankTracker, 28 Dec. 2022, https://www.mybanktracker.com/savings/faq/how-to-set-up-a-savings-account-for-a-teenager-297534#:~:text=Minor's%20can%20only%20open%20a,long%20as%20it%20is%20open

8. "Investing for Teens: 9 Ways to Get Your Teen Started." *The Dough Roller*, https://www.doughroller.net/investing/best-investments-for-teens/

9. "7 Steps to Investing as a Teenager [in 2023]." *TeenVestor*, https://www.teenvestor.com/7steps

10. Paulus, Nathan. "How to Build a Personal Finance Foundation for Teens." *MoneyGeek.com*, MoneyGeek.com, 12 Dec. 2022, https://www.moneygeek.com/financial-planning/personal-finance-for-teens/

11. "Money Management Tips for Teens." *Credit Counselling Society*, 2 Feb. 2023, https://nomoredebts.org/budgeting/budgeting-for-teens

CHAPTER 7

1. Maze, Victor. "Inspiring Quotes to Motivate You to Start Cleaning and Decluttering." *Veranda*, 3 June 2022, https://www.veranda.com/home-decorators/g32031382/decluttering-cleaning-quotes/

2. "Who 'Golden Rules' for Safe Food Preparation." *PAHO/WHO | Pan American Health Organization*, https://www.paho.org/en/health-emergencies/who-golden-rules-safe-food-preparation

3. Center for Food Safety and Applied Nutrition. "Food Safety in Your Kitchen." *U.S. Food and Drug Administration*, FDA, https://www.fda.gov/food/buy-store-serve-safe-food/food-safety-your-kitchen

4. "Kitchen Hygiene and Food Safety." *Safefood*, https://www.safefood.net/food-safety/kitchen-hygiene

5. The Jakarta Post. "7 Things You Should Never Heat in the Microwave." *The Jakarta Post*, https://www.thejakartapost.com/life/2019/06/09/7-things-you-should-never-heat-in-the-microwave.html

6. "First Aid Tips for Kitchen Accidents." *WebMD*, WebMD, https://www.webmd.com/first-aid/kitchen-first-aid

7. Leverette, Mary Marlowe. "Laundry Hampered? How to Do Laundry in 10 Easy Steps." *The Spruce*, The Spruce, 5 July 2022, https://www.thespruce.com/how-to-do-laundry-2146149

8. Leverette, Mary Marlowe. "Learn How to Unshrink a Shrunken Sweater." *The Spruce*, The Spruce, 1 Dec. 2022, https://www.thespruce.com/saving-a-shrunken-wool-sweater-2146669

9. Johnson.Editor.Sew4Home, Liz. "How to Sew on a Button by Hand." *Sew4Home*, 20 Feb. 2022, https://sew4home.com/how-to-sew-on-a-button-by-hand/

10. "First-Aid Kit (for Parents) - Nemours Kidshealth." Edited by Melanie L. Pitone, *KidsHealth*, The Nemours Foundation, June 2022, https://kidshealth.org/en/parents/firstaid-kit.html

11. "First Aid Tips: How to Treat Burns, Cuts, and Bites." *WebMD*, WebMD, https://www.webmd.com/first-aid/first-aid-tips

12. Mills, Chris. "CPR & First Aid for Teens in Raleigh." *CPR Educators, Inc.*, 20 July 2020, https://cpreducatorsinc.com/cpr-first-aid-tips-for-teens/

13. Krans, Brian. "Heimlich Maneuver: How to Perform and When to Use It." *Healthline*, Healthline Media, 4 Aug. 2017, https://www.healthline.com/health/heimlich-maneuver#steps

14. "Sprain: First Aid." *Mayo Clinic*, Mayo Foundation for Medical Education and Research, 22 Mar. 2022, https://www.mayoclinic.org/first-aid/first-aid-sprain/basics/art-20056622

15. "Concussion." *Mayo Clinic*, Mayo Foundation for Medical Education and Research, 17 Feb. 2022, https://www.

mayoclinic.org/diseases-conditions/concussion/symptoms-causes/syc-20355594

CHAPTER 8

1. "Your Body Is like a Car Quote: Body, Take Care of Your Body, Inspirational Quotes." *Pinterest*, 19 Aug. 2019, https://www.pinterest.com/pin/your-body-is-like-a-car-quote--260082947217268512/

2. Dolman Law Group Accident Injury Lawyers, PA. "30 Teen Driving Statistics and Safe Driving Facts." *Dolman Law Group*, 11 Apr. 2022, https://www.dolmanlaw.com/blog/teen-driving-statistics/

3. "Teen Driver and Passenger Safety." *Centers for Disease Control and Prevention*, Centers for Disease Control and Prevention, 21 Nov. 2022, https://www.cdc.gov/transportationsafety/teen_drivers/index.html

4. "Teen Driving Statistics." *RMIIA*, http://www.rmiia.org/auto/teens/Teen_Driving_Statistics.asp

5. "Behind the Wheel: How to Help Your Teen Become a Safe Driver." *HealthyChildren.org*, https://healthychildren.org/English/ages-stages/teen/safety/Pages/Behind-the-Wheel-Helping-Teens-Become-Safe-Drivers.aspx

6. Reed, Philip. "10 Things Teens Should Know about Cars and Driving." *Edmunds*, 29 Sept. 2011, https://www.edmunds.com/car-news/tips-advice/10-things-teens-should-know-about-cars-and-driving.html

7. Burke, Christine. "My Kids Are Living Their Best Lives While I'm behind the Wheel-Your Teen Mag." *Your Teen Magazine*, 29 Sept. 2021, https://yourteenmag.com/teenager-school/teens-high-school/always-driving

8. Fenyo, Erica. "A Teen Driver's Guide to Getting Pulled Over." *The Coat of Arms*, https://menlocoa.org/20925/a-and-l/a-teen-drivers-guide-to-getting-pulled-over/

9. Simeon, Diana. "How to Handle Getting Pulled over by a Policeman - Your Teen Mag." *Your Teen Magazine*, 4 May 2021, https://yourteenmag.com/teenager-school/teens-high-school/parents-teen-driving/driving-expert-advice

Printed in Great Britain
by Amazon